Sheila's Shop

Sheila's Shop

Working-Class African American Women Talk about Life, Love, Race, and Hair

Kimberly Battle-Walters

ROWMAN & LITTLEFIELD PUBLISHERS, INC.
Lanham • Boulder • New York • Toronto • Oxford

ROWMAN & LITTLEFIELD PUBLISHERS, INC.

Published in the United States of America
by Rowman & Littlefield Publishers, Inc.
A wholly owned subsidary of The Rowman & Littlefield Publishing Group, Inc.
4501 Forbes Boulevard, Suite 200, Lanham, MD 20706
www.rowmanlittlefield.com

P.O. Box 317, Oxford OX2 9RU, UK

British Library Cataloguing in Publication Information Available

Library of Congress Cataloging-in-Publication Data

Battle-Walters, Kimberly, 1967–
  Sheila's shop : working-class African American women talk about life, love, race, and
hair / Kimberly Battle-Walters.
      p. cm.
  Includes bibliographical references and index.
  ISBN 0-8476-9932-3 (cloth : alk. paper) — ISBN 0-8476-9933-1 (pbk. :
alk. paper)
  1. African American women—Social conditions. 2. Working class
women—United States—Social conditions. 3. African American
women—Interviews. 4. Working class women—United States—Interviews.
5. Social networks—United States. 6. Community life—United States.
7. Stress (Psychology)—United States. 8. African American families.
9. Racism—United States. 10. United States—Race relations. I.
Title.
  E185.86.B376 2004
  305.48'896073—dc22
                                                          2004000451

Printed in the United States of America

∞™ The paper used in this publication meets the minimum requirements of
American National Standard for Information Sciences—Permanence of Paper for
Printed Library Materials, ANSI/NISO Z39.48-1992.

To the women of Sheila's shop who were resourceful and resilient;
Janet Walters and Estella Tillman; my mother and grandmother—
two of the most amazing working-class African American women that I know;
and to David L. Tillman, my grandfather, who planted the seed
for the name of my new theoretical concept.

Contents

Introduction

Great civilizations, like great cities, share a common feature. Evolving within them and crucial to their growth and refinement are distinctive informal public gathering places. These become as much a part of the urban landscape as of the citizen's daily life and, invariably, they come to dominate the image of the city. . . . Where urban growth proceeds with no indigenous version of a public gathering place proliferated along the way and integral in the lives of the people, the promise of the city is denied. Without such places, the urban area fails to nourish the kinds of relationships and the diversity of human contact that are the essence of the city. Deprived of these settings, people remain lonely within their crowds.

—Ray Oldenburg, *The Great Good Place*

Sociologists fail to acknowledge the historical strength of the black working and lower working classes, creating the impression that without middle-class and even upper working-class respectability the black community is devoid of its moral base.

—Mitchell Duneier, *Slim's Table*

What is it like to be a working-class African American woman today? The opening quotes address this question and encapsulate the focus of this book: the lives of working-class Black women, as told in public gatherings such as a Black beauty shop. As a working-class African American woman who wanted to observe the lives of other working-class African American women, I

1

needed to identify a place where this type of woman gathers and nourishes her relationships. As stipulated in Oldenburg's quote, informal public gathering places are essential to the cultivation of support networks. This is especially the case in Black communities, where a sense of ownership and familiarity is frequently sought out. I identified the Black beauty shop as one such gathering place. Social scientists over the last decade have identified beauty shops as key social and informational centers. This has become especially evident within Black communities, where solidarity can sometimes feel lost.[1]

Beyond the fact that I am a working-class African American woman, why did I choose to look at other *working-class* African American women? The answer is simple: There is a scarcity of literature that describes the life experiences of working-class African American women. Much of the literature focuses on the "pathologies" of poor urban African Americans, reinforcing stereotypical images. And works that portray the plight of African American women on welfare have been well cited in both scholarly and popular culture literature.[2] Pictures of the single Black mother are vividly etched in our minds, while images of successful working-class African American women are not routinely produced. The lack of the former helps further embellish stereotypes, creating the illusion that poor and working-class Blacks have little to no initiative or morals or that they need the motivation and mores of mainstream society to "show them the way."

Other studies showcase the achievements or progress of African Americans, thereby playing down continuous racial inequities altogether.[3] Written works that examine the Black middle-class experience of both men and women, such as *Living with Racism* by Joe Feagin and Melvin Sikes and *The Rage of a Privileged Class* by Ellis Cose, exist. However, studies that focus exclusively on the experiences of working-class Black women are limited.[4]

It was for this reason that I conducted in-depth interviews and intricately observed the lives of twenty African American women in a southern beauty shop over an extended period. I discuss the role that the beauty shop played in helping facilitate support networks for the women throughout the book, as well as in affecting the lives of the women who frequented this beauty shop.

The central goal of this book is to describe working-class African American women's "lived experiences."[5] These women are the experts of their own lives, and my part as the author and researcher has been to record and present their experiences, using their voices. These women discuss their lives, express their views, and tell their stories united in one voice, empowered by many voices, voices that have historically been ignored.

Given the limited amount of literature on the everyday existence of working-class African American women, particularly that which examines their lives within indigenous social structures, such as Black beauty shops, I have tried to examine the lives of these women from a holistic perspective. This approach required looking at how specific parts of these women's lives affected them as a whole. For example, how did being Black affect who they were as women? Or, what support networks did these women have? Answering these and other questions involved looking at aspects of these women's social, political, economic, and religious ideologies.

The African American women in this book are given the opportunity to describe their everyday lived experiences, highlighting race, gender, and class issues. Emerging from these three areas are comments regarding public misconceptions about them, relational issues, and common stereotypes that have perpetuated degrading images of African American women both individually and collectively. In keeping consistent with the women, I use the terms *Black* and *African American* intermittently to include those who are Black but not originally American as well as those who can be identified as African American but refer to themselves as Black.

To get to know these women better, I interviewed them individually over sixteen months. In addition to tape-recorded interviews, I wrote down my personal observations of the women and their surroundings and tape-recorded several informal beauty shop group discussions about local and national events. I changed the names of the women to protect their identities and sought to protect them further by sometimes quoting them without stating even their aliases. This was particularly the case when statements made by the women could potentially jeopardize a personal or professional relationship.

The four main questions that the women discuss and answer throughout the book are:

What is it like to be a working-class African American woman in America today?

How do working-class African American women view the status of Black families and Black communities?

What are working-class African American women's perceptions of race relations?

How do working-class African American women cope with everyday life pressures?

I chose to ask questions, as opposed to starting out with predetermined conclusions, for I wanted the women to tell me who they were themselves, independent of how I or society saw them. I wanted to give them, and only them, the opportunity to dispel any socially inflicted myths—so much so that

I originally entitled this manuscript *Dispelling the Myth: The Experiences and Realities of Working-Class African American Women*.

In considering the questions just listed, the first question examines what it is like to be an African American woman. This question seeks to answer how these women see themselves within the context of their racial background, gender, and socioeconomic class. It looks at the degree to which race affects gender and gender affects race, as well as at the women's perceptions of how the media portray Black women. This question also allows the women to describe their perceived similarities to and differences from White women. This question is discussed in chapter 2.

The second question asks the women to describe their feelings and concerns about the status of Black families and communities. Their views on the strengths and weaknesses of their communities are discussed, as well as practical ways to ameliorate community problems. In answering this question, the women also speak about their individual relationships with Black men and Black women. This discussion is found in chapter 3.

The third question looks at working-class African American women's generalized perceptions of current racial relations in America. It seeks to understand the current status of racial relations from the point of view of the women. Their perceptions of whether racial relations have become better or worse are addressed. The women's experiences with racism and discrimination also are noted, and the women give their views on affirmative action and whether it is still needed today. These issues are all discussed in chapter 4.

In considering the final question, addressed in chapter 5, the women describe how working-class Black women cope with everyday life pressures. Often facing overwhelming odds, these women relate how they not only survive but also thrive. The women acknowledge and elaborate on family, community, and religious supports. They speak about the goals and accomplishments that they have achieved in spite of various challenges, as well as what percentage of any given day they spend thinking about racism, sexism, and classism.

Profiles of the Community and the Women

Since 2000, the southern city in which the shop is located has grown to a population of over a hundred thousand, more than double its size during the time of my interviews. However, racial data for this city have remained largely consistent, with three-fourths of the population being White and the remaining fourth being made up primarily by Blacks. Women are still in the majority, making up approximately 52 percent of the city's population, and over half of the city's population is over the age of twenty-five. Although many people living on the outskirts of this city were economically well-to-do, according to the *U.S. Census of Population and Housing for Florida* in 1990, the majority of households in the vicinity of the beauty shop, which were predominately African American, reported incomes between $5,000 and $9,999, indicating local poverty. By 2000, the household incomes in the same community had only risen to between $15,000 and the low $20,000s annually.

The number of single African American men between the ages of twenty and seventy-four was approximately 25 percent less than that of single African American women in this city. As the gap between the number of single Black women and single Black men increased, the number of single Black women and single Black heads of households increased. This helps account for the number of Black female-headed households with children under the age of eighteen, which was more than double that of Black married-couple households with children under eighteen years of age.

Within this community, each of the women that I interviewed came from a working-class background. People from working-class backgrounds were identified as those who had household incomes between $15,000 and $35,000 a year during the late 1990s. Generally, people of working-class economic status have little or no accumulated wealth, work in blue-collar jobs with minimal, if any, insurance benefits, and are extremely vulnerable to financial problems resulting from illnesses or temporary unemployment.[6] While college is often seen as a lofty goal, only about one-third of working-class youth actually are able to go to college.

Although all of the women came from working-class backgrounds, and the median household income of the twenty women was $23,500, a fourth of the women had recently moved up the economic ladder to what could be classified as a middle-class status. This included those women who had gone on to white-collar jobs, who had combined household salaries of over $35,000 a year, or who had completed at least a four-year college degree. And while only a few of the women fell into this category, the majority (two-thirds) had done well enough to purchase their own homes.

The women in the shop were between the ages of twenty and seventy. Out of the twenty women, five had never been married, seven were married, and eight were divorced and had not remarried. With one exception, each of the married women and those who had been married had at least one child, but only one of the single never-married women had had children. This is especially significant in light of the stereotype of Black women as promiscuous and having several children out of wedlock, which is also contrary to more recent national statistics.

The education levels of these women ranged from a tenth-grade education to a master's degree. Eighteen of the twenty women had at least a high school diploma with some college experience, with the average number of years of postsecondary education being 2.3 years. All twenty of these women were registered voters.

Each woman identified herself with a religious denomination; these included religious experiences from Pentecostal/Holiness, Baptist, and Seventh-Day Adventist backgrounds. This being said, although each woman associated herself with a religious denomination, not every woman attended church regularly.

Methods

I gained access to this particular shop and established rapport with these women through church affiliations, which have been known to be a key resource within the Black community.[7] With the permission of Sheila, the shop owner, I posted a flyer in the beauty shop informing her clients of my study. The women who were interested in participating in the study were given a sign-up sheet on which to leave their names and phone numbers so that I could contact them and schedule interviews.

As a participant–observer who also did open-ended, face-to-face interviews, I drew a purposive nonprobability sample of women who best fit the focus of my study. The beauty shop environment provided a perfect public place to meet and dialogue with a pool of working-class Black women and a safe haven in which personal and social information could be shared. Gathering information was facilitated by the fact that the women were confined to this setting, by choice, for a minimum of two hours while getting their hair done. This gave me a captive audience of women who were willing to participate in my study as a way of minimizing their waiting time.

As a working-class African American woman, I discovered several benefits to doing face-to-face, open-ended interviews. These interviews allowed me to observe nonverbal cues and gave the women the opportunity to describe their own experiences with someone of a similar background. Even though I had a graduate degree, the women trusted me as a woman of color who shared a working-class background like theirs. I was not just a researcher in their eyes but a friend, and I have remained in contact with Sheila and many of the women.

I actively engaged in "shop talk" with the women that included the everyday life happenings of these women and discussions of current social problems. These conversations helped me to establish a good rapport with the women, creating an environment in which they felt comfortable sharing specific life experiences with me. Our exchanges also allowed me to gain a well-rounded view of the women whom I interviewed. During our talks, I used the same southern Black colloquialisms as the women in the shop, a language neither contrived nor premeditated but very spontaneous and natural. This colloquial change happens to many Blacks when they are talking to each other, unlike when conversing with a person of another race. Feeling comfortable and safe with each other, many Blacks, as well as other people of color, tend to slide into a comfortable slang that is more relaxed than their formal and professional vocabulary.

Making biweekly visits to the shop, I began my interviews and participation in November 1995 and ended in March 1997; I returned to the shop for some follow-up information during the spring of 1999. Although over half of the interviews were done within the first twelve months, much of my time in the shop was spent establishing a relationship and rapport with the women by engaging in shop talk and observing client relationships as a participant.

Upon developing a trusted friendship with Sheila, the owner of the shop, and her family, I was soon invited to stay in their home on the weekends that I came in town to do interviews. These weekend stays made my visits twice a month comfortable, relaxed, and time-efficient. This was especially the case when scheduled interviews were canceled and additional interviews were not scheduled until the next day.

Central Paradigm and Theoretical Concepts

I centered these women's stories on the lived experiences paradigm. In the lived experiences model, one's personal story and experiences are more important than the social issue or problem that is being addressed. The individual is the expert of his or her own experience, not the researcher. Hence, I allowed the women's lived experiences to shape theory rather than permitting theory to shape their experiences.

Within the lived experiences paradigm, I drew consistently upon three racial relations theoretical concepts. The following three concepts were used to help explore and interpret the everyday life experiences of these working-class African American women: gendered racism, cumulative lived experiences, and "the habit of surviving."[8] I focused on racial relations theoretical concepts, because I was primarily interested in how race affected the women's perceptions of themselves and their views of the larger social structure, as well as how their race affected their gender and class.

In the first theoretical model, Philomena Essed conceptualizes the inter-action between racial and gender oppression as gendered racism. This concept examines the relationship between race and gender. Essed defines this concept as "the racial oppression of Black women as structured by racist and ethnicist perceptions of gender roles."[9] She suggests that the social status of being a woman is further complicated by racial hegemony. According to Essed, being both Black and female is a double burden. An example of this would be the lower wages that Black women receive as a result of being both Black and female.

Essed also points out that gendered racism accounts for the media images that portray Black women as being either Aunt Jemimas or sexually promiscuous. This perspective may be evident in classic television and movie roles that have traditionally cast Black women as cheerful maids or wanton seducers.

When looking specifically at the gender aspect of gendered racism, Essed points out that Black working-class women are often measured against White middle-class women's standards, in relationship to beauty, family structure, and feminist stance. As a result of their strength and high endurance levels, Essed suggests, Black women are sometimes not seen as women, in comparison to White women. Somehow the fragility or beauty associated with White women is excluded from the image of Black women. This idea is explored more when I examine how working-class Black women see themselves in relation to White women.

When looking at the racial component of gendered racism, Essed says that Black women are often put at odds against their Black male counterparts. Black women are often accused of taking jobs away from Black men and dislocating Black men from their roles as heads of households. The gendered racism concept is used to further explore the effects of gender and race on Black male and female relationships. This point is examined more in the chapter on Black families and communities.

The second theoretical concept, the cumulative lived experiences, states that "the cumulative impact on an individual of repeated personal encounters with racial hostility is greater than the sum of these encounters might appear to be to a casual observer."[10] This theoretical concept proposes that it is not so much the sporadic incidents of racism that are individually monumental but rather the sum of a lifetime of racism and discrimination that plays a big part in many Blacks' outlook and anger.

This concept supports the idea that in dealing with cumulative racist experiences, Blacks often share their experiences of racism with their family members. This changes individual experiences with racism into a family or communal experience with racism. Aspects of recent and past discrimination become merged. These events are then stored in the memories of the individual, his or her friends, family members, and the larger community. When it comes to a particular incident, the details of the event no longer belong solely to the individual, to whom the event happened, but rather turn into a communal experience ingrained in the memories of all those who heard about the event. Individual experiences are transformed into communal experiences through a process in which events are shared and remembered, known as "collective memory."[11] This collective memory assists Blacks in coping with blatant racism by allowing other supportive family members and friends to share in the individual's painful experience vicariously.

Even with familial support, repeated experiences with racism greatly affect the way Blacks perceive and react to social situations. Joe Feagin and Melvin Sikes state that Blacks ultimately develop what they identify as "the second eye." This means that African Americans often have to ask themselves whether what they perceive to be discrimination is merely an oversight that could happen to anyone or an intentional act of racism.

Finally, this concept points out that the daily experiences of racial hostility and discrimination experienced by Blacks are part of a larger tapestry of socially condoned hegemony known as "institutional racism." I use the cumulative lived experiences concept to examine how all forms of racism affect these women's everyday life perceptions, existence, and opportunities.

The third concept that I utilize to explore the lives of these African American women is one that Kesho Yvonne Scott identifies as "the habit of surviving." Scott defines this theoretical concept as "the external adjustments and internal adaptations that people make to [survive] economic exploitation and racial and gender-related oppression."[12] She explains that African American women have learned a host of strategies to cope with external social pressures such as racism, sexism, and classism. Sometimes these strategies are self-imposed, and other times these strategies are passed down to them from their mothers and other women in their families and social circles. These strategies become habitual responses to pain and suffering that help them to lessen their anger and gain hope.

The "warrior mode" is one such habit that Scott identifies. The warrior mode is explained as "an attitude, a style of approaching life, in which one perceives existence as a continuous battle."[13] This habit consists of facing life events much like one would a battle. According to Scott, this warrior mode accounts for Black women feeling like they are responsible for carrying the weight of the world on their shoulders. They often feel like they have to be superwomen, battling the forces of everyday life. Other strategies that Black women sometimes use include ignoring or laughing at discriminatory acts or comments. These varied responses are related to resisting or in some cases adapting to socially condoned mistreatment.

Scott points out that the habit of surviving at times causes those who are oppressed to unknowingly engage in behaviors that often perpetuate their racial, gender, or class oppression. An example of this is when a Black woman accepts the dominant culture's stereotypes of her and acts them out unconsciously (e.g., hip hop queen, ghetto girl). At other times, Black women may knowingly comply with an oppressive system to shield themselves or others from anticipated painful and discriminatory situations. An example of this would be a Black woman purposely acting subservient to a White supervisor in order to be perceived as nonthreatening, because she experienced trouble in her last job for being too outspoken. This concept is useful when examining how survival habits can ultimately inhibit African American women's personal growth and foster false adaptation rather than promoting positive racial, gender, and economic changes.[14]

The Extended Case Method

In reviewing both my conversations with the women and my shop observations, I used the extended case method to examine the application of these three racial relations concepts. The extended case method, according to Michael Burawoy, "seeks generalization through reconstructing existing generalizations, that is, the reconstruction of existing theory."[15] Simply stated, this method constructs new theory from existing theory. Instead of trying to explain a phenomenon with existing theory, the extended case method allows the phenomenon to help reshape existing theory and thereby create new theory. Unlike grounded theory, which seeks to discover new theory by abstracting phenomenon from time and place, the extended case method focuses on revising applicable existing theory.[16]

I must emphasize that the purpose of the extended case method is not to determine statistical significance numerically, such as with large random sample sizes, but rather to understand the experiential significance of a few. I used the extended case method to focus on both the significance that could be found in the experiences of these twenty women and what they told me about the larger social environment in which they lived. The generalizability of these women's experiences is made as other working-class African American women around the country concur with what these twenty women expressed, through confirmation with existing studies, and through comparing these women to other Black women and working-class women of different races.

In chapters 2 through 5, I apply the three racial relations concepts and consider their usefulness in addressing my four key questions. In the final chapter, however, I revisit these existing theoretical concepts and then impose a new theoretical insight based on what I learned from these women. If you listen closely, you, too, will find that these women have something to teach us all.

Notes

1. Darryl E. Owens, "Hair Care Comes with Prayers," *Orlando Sentinel*, April 22, 2000, D1, D8; Audrey Edwards, "Programs That Work: Looking Good . . . Inside and Out," *Essence* 27 (April 1997): 50; Michael Krikorian, "Central Los Angeles: Along with Mousse, Salon Offers AIDS and Cancer Advice," *Los Angeles Times*, May 16, 1997, 5; Aisha Mori, "Letting Their Hair Down," *San Gabriel Valley Weekly*, June 8, 2001, 1, 8.

2. See Daniel Patrick Moynihan, *The Negro Family* (Washington, D.C.: U.S. Department of Labor, 1965); Charles Murray, *Losing Ground: American Social Policy, 1950–1980* (New York: West, 1984); Richard Hernstein and Charles Murray, *The Bell Curve* (New York: Free Press, 1994); Robin L. Jarrett, "Living Poor: Family Life among Single Parent, African American Women," *Social Problems* 41 (1994): 30–49; Robin L. Jarrett, "Welfare Stigma among Low-Income African American Single Mothers," *Family Relations* 45 (1996): 368–74; Richard Caputo, "Family Poverty, Unemployment Rates, and AFDC Payments: Trends among Blacks and Whites," *Families in Society: The Journal of Contemporary Human Services* 74 (1993): 515–25; Jill Quadagno, *The Color of Welfare: How Racism Undermines the War on Poverty* (New York: Oxford University Press, 1994); Karen Seccombe, Delores James, and Kimberly Battle-Walters, "They Think You Ain't Much of Nothing: The Social Construction of the Welfare Mother," *Journal of Marriage and the Family* 60 (1998): 849–65.

3. Ben Wattenberg and Richard Scammon, "Black Progress and Liberal Rhetoric," *Commentary* (April 1973): 35; Nathan Glazer, *Affirmative Discrimination* (New York: Basic Books, 1975).

4. Kesho Yvonne Scott, *The Habit of Surviving: Black Women's Strategies for Life* (New Brunswick, N.J.: Rutgers University Press, 1991); Philomena Essed, *Everyday Racism* (Claremont, Calif.: Hunter House, 1990); Lois Benjamin, *The Black Elite: Facing the Color Line in the Twilight of the Twentieth Century* (Chicago: Nelson-Hall, 1991); Yanick St. Jean and Joe R. Feagin, *Double Burden: Black Women and Everyday Racism* (Armonk, N.Y.: Sharpe, 1997); Lois Rita Helmbold, "Writing the History of Black and White Working Class Women," *Women's Studies* 17 (1989): 37–48; Linda M. Blum and Theresa Deussen, "Negotiating Independent Motherhood: Working-Class African American Women Talk about Marriage and Motherhood," *Gender & Society* 10 (1996): 199–211.

5. The concept of lived experiences is used to examine the personal insights, experiences, and stories that the women bring. See Joe R. Feagin and Melvin P. Sikes, *Living with Racism: The Black Middle-Class Experience* (Boston: Beacon, 1994); Angela

McBride and William McBride, "Theoretical Underpinnings for Women's Health," *Women and Health* 6 (1981): 37–55.

6. John J. Macionis, *Sociology*, 6th ed. (Upper Saddle River, N.J.: Prentice Hall, 1997).

7. Black churches are key social, political, and informative sources within Black communities. See K. Sue Jewell, *Survival of the Black Family* (New York: Praeger, 1988).

8. For gendered racism, see Philomena Essed, *Understanding Everyday Racism* (Newbury Park, Calif.: Sage, 1991); for cumulative lived experiences, see Feagan and Sikes, *Living with racism*; for the "habit of surviving," see Scott, *The Habit of Surviving*.

9. Essed, *Understanding Everyday Racism*, 31.

10. Feagin and Sikes, *Living with Racism*, 16.

11. Maurice Halbwachs, *The Collective Memory* (New York: Harper & Row, 1980).

12. Scott, *The Habit of Surviving*, 7.

13. Scott, *The Habit of Surviving*, 8.

14. The extended case method looks at how existing theoretical concepts explain a given phenomenon. I used it to evaluate the effectiveness of the three racial theoretical concepts in helping one to understand the lived experiences of the women in this study. This method is later used to introduce a fourth conceptual component of the lived experiences paradigm.

15. Michael Burawoy, *Ethnography Unbound* (Berkeley: University of California Press, 1991), 279.

16. For grounded theory, see Barney G. Glaser and Anselm L. Strauss, *The Discovery of Grounded Theory* (New York: Aldine de Gruyter, 1967).

CHAPTER ONE

Sheila's Shop

> Everything I know about American history I learned from looking at black people's hair. . . . It's all in the hair.
>
> —Lisa Jones, *Bulletproof Diva*

In a southern city with a population that is not too big, but big enough, sits a small white building on the corner of a busy highway. This white building is not just any building, but a source of refuge for some and a hope for new beginnings for others. In this bustling working-class Black neighborhood, this inconspicuous building serves as a gathering place for African American women. In it they visit, share their stories, and debate world events as they wait to get their hair done. This place is known as "the shop," the beauty shop, Sheila's shop.

Sheila's shop sits catty-corner from a funeral home, down the street from a local National Association for the Advancement of Colored People office, and in the same block as an auto parts store. Just around the corner from the shop are several low-income houses occupied by people who seem to be enjoying the simple joys of life, despite their economic limitations. For example, on any given weekend night, the neighborhood turns into what seems to be one big block party.

Sheila's shop, named after its owner, is in close proximity to seemingly more sophisticated hair salons, but none seem to be quite as busy or as loved as Sheila's. The smallness of Sheila's two-room shop does not lend itself to a large business clientele, but it is precisely this smallness that keeps customers coming back. The small building initiates fellowship, promotes a sense of community, and fosters intimate friendships. For this, women come from near and far to get their hair done, because Sheila's shop is not only a beauty shop but also a place that feels like home.

With the area having a reputation for criminal activity, as a safety precaution clients have become well acquainted with knocking on a securely locked door to gain entrance to the beauty shop. Upon entering the shop, clients are immediately embraced by warm greetings from Sheila, other friendly customers, and the warm shop air that is generated by the stationary dryers. The aroma of fried hair permeates the atmosphere. And although this smell and heat could be cause for concern to a newcomer, for those who frequent the shop, they are hardly even noticeable.

The shop decor consists of white walls with splashes of black paint to offset the matching black cabinets and the black-and-white checkered floor. Pictures of hairstyles cover the walls, providing ideas for clients who come without any certainty as to how they want their locks done. No cash register is in sight. Although this is a place of business, the sight of a register would appear too businesslike for this relaxed atmosphere.

The shop is a haven for the women who patronize it. For at least two hours each month, these women find refuge and support without the cares or concerns of their families, jobs, or communities. If only for a while, in the shop these women can take a break from their demanding roles as mothers, wives, and workers and finally catch their breath. Shop time is their time. With it they can choose to talk or just be pampered, but, more important, they can count on being heard.

Two hair styling chairs sit in front of one large mirror, and directly across from the styling chairs are three bright orange seats, reflecting the 1970s motif, for waiting clients. No more than three feet away from the styling chairs and the waiting area are two shampoo and rinsing chairs, with only one sink being regularly used. To the right of the two shampoo chairs is a bathroom that seems relatively large for this small, cozy setting. In an adjacent room there are four stationary dryers. These four dryers are all going at any given time, "cooking" the women's hair and scalps. Although entering the dryer room is a necessary part of the hair process, most women wince at the thought of baking under this tremendous heat. Near the dryers are three stacks of fashion and popular magazines to help divert the women's attention from the heat and the wait. In the corner of the dryer room is a door that leads to an adjacent apartment that is rented by Sheila's relatives at various times and used by Sheila at her discretion at other times. This room is off-limits to clients and is not really considered part of the shop, thereby limiting the scope of the shop to two rooms.

The Women

Among the shop patrons is a core group of women who bond in the shop as well as outside the shop. Sheila, the shop's only stylist, gently nurtures this core group similar to the way a mother would care for her children. A tall, robust woman who speaks with authority, Sheila has an element of gentleness that keeps her patrons confiding in her and coming back. As a single, thirty-something Black woman, Sheila is quite articulate and vocal when it comes to politics, social problems, and her religious beliefs. She strongly supports postsecondary education, even though she herself does not have a college degree. Although she has been at this location for only a few years, she has known and cared for some of her clients for over a decade. This seems to be consistent with other findings that suggest that patrons are extremely loyal when a beautician is good.[1]

Jean and Priscilla are two of Sheila's regulars at the shop. Since Priscilla does not have a car, she usually catches a ride with Jean for Saturday morning appointments. Priscilla, a full-time student, plans her visits to the shop much like one would plan a very important meeting. This five foot, spunky twenty-something looks forward to her Saturday visits. For her, it is a time to get a new style and also a time to hang out with the older and wiser women to learn important lessons in life. Priscilla grows weary of her hairstyles after only a few days. The fact that she has to have a new style each week keeps Priscilla coming back and makes her one of Sheila's regular clients.

Jean, a calm, unassuming woman, usually soaks up shop conversation, listening more than actually talking until something sparks her fancy. Jean's soothing personality usually causes her to act as the peacemaker and the optimist when shop discussions turn unpleasant. As a teacher of students with disabilities, Jean usually supports the underdog.

Since Sheila works alone, she frequently receives help in the afternoons from her sister-in-law Burnadette. As a young mother of five, Burnadette frequently uses the shop as a solace and way to escape her motherly responsibilities. Known for her lack of cooking abilities, "Burn"adette is often the brunt of cruel cooking jokes. Some days Burnadette handles these jokes better than others.

Jackie, who has been a regular Friday customer for years, is quite outspoken and opinionated. As an older woman, Jackie has seen and experienced too much of life to be shy. Whether it is politics or relationships, Jackie always has something to say, and she often speaks loudly when saying it. The other women have learned to patiently give Jackie her time to talk when she's on a roll and subtly move on to another topic when she lets up.

Then there is Sassy. Sassy is Sheila's younger sister. This recently married mother is known for her expensive taste and impulsive shopping sprees. What Sassy wants, Sassy gets! Her independent nature periodically clashes with Sheila's more nurturing and motherly personality; however, these two never let any animosity divide them. Even when they do not see eye to eye, they find a way to move past opinions to support one another. This is also true of the other core patrons. A sisterly type love and support seem to be more important than minor disagreements. When disagreements or conflicts come up, the women quickly change the topic of discussion or use humor to disarm the tension.

Finally there is Mother Mac, Sheila's mom. Mother Mac is a very soft-spoken woman who is generous in nature. A fair and pleasantly plump woman, she has a warm smile, a caring heart, and is concerned about a stranger just as much as she is her own family. Raising several foster children in addition to her own biological children with her hardworking husband, Mother Mac has a lot of love to give and doesn't get bogged down with minor details like whether one is biologically related.

The women genuinely care about each other, and this was evident in their generosity to each other and their regular contact with each other throughout the week. These women saw each other in the beauty shop, at church, talked to each other on the phone, and ate in each other's homes. If one was sick or discouraged, the group checked to see if they could do anything, including helping out financially. The group is truly a sisterhood.

Some of the other clients who frequented the shop but were not necessarily a part of this core group included Berniece, an outspoken minister's wife who endured a difficult past as a single parent on welfare, prior to becoming the "first lady" of her church; Ms. Foster, a politically and socially informed middle-aged woman who listened carefully to others before she gently inserted her words of wisdom; Donna, a college student with strong religious convictions, whose charismatic expressions seemed to frighten both her boyfriend and those who got within arms distance of her; and Miss Mary, a seventy-year-old woman of Caribbean ancestry who prided herself in having a successful marriage of over fifty years and raising a son who received a doctorate, even though she herself did not complete high school. These women were all varied, interesting, and inspiring.

My role with the previously mentioned core group of women was quite unique. As an outsider coming in, my challenge was both to develop and maintain trusted relationships with the women whom I would later interview, and to remain objective as I interviewed them and gathered important information about their everyday lived experiences. While trying to negotiate this delicate balance, I gradually became a part of this core network after spending much time with Sheila and her family. As an out-of-towner away from home, I was adopted by Sheila and her relatives as fictive kin, making me a part of their family while I was away from my own.

As somewhat of a little sister or mascot to the core group of women in the shop, I was frequently invited to spend time with these women's families, including being invited to eat meals with them. This proved useful to my frugal budget and helpful in terms of my understanding of the bond between this core group of clients that went beyond the shop. It also proved useful in terms of getting hair discounts. The core group of women received a special discount when it came to hair prices. Although most of Sheila's clients paid about $35 for a visit to the shop, the core group members paid about $25.

The women in the shop were known for their strong opinions and lack of timidity. Their conversations varied greatly both in context and intensity. Conversations often went from personal problems to social crises in a matter of minutes.

> The television announces, "Identical twins have kids by the same man! On the next *Montel.*"
> SHEILA: Oh, I heard about that. That's a shame!
> KIM: Were these girls Black?
> SHEILA: No, thank God, but we're getting that crazy, too!
> JACKIE: We are portrayed more negatively in the media than anybody else. People always associate bad things with Blacks. I heard about this sixteen-year-old girl who had three kids. It's a shame! (She stops her discussion to direct Sheila on how to cut her hair.)
> SHEILA: I have a problem with the system. I think they need to come up with a way to adjudicate these bad kids, because HRS [a social service office] don't want you to do nothing to them, and so these kids act out, hitting you, kicking . . . .
> JACKIE: I prefer birth control be taught in school than them going out and getting pregnant.
> SHEILA: A lot of these girls know about birth control, but they still go out and get pregnant.
> KIM: Why do you think that is? (addressed toward Sheila)
> JACKIE: (Jumps in before Sheila can answer) We need to stop giving out welfare. Because after the second child it wasn't a mistake—it's a habit!
> SHEILA: You are being too nice, because I say after the first.
> JACKIE: You're right! I only get paid every two weeks. I'm tired of big chunks of my paycheck going out to these kids that don't work. These dads need to . . . .

SHEILA: Can't they untie your tubes? They should do that [tie their tubes] for girls with kids.

KIM: When they were giving the Norplant to Black teenagers up north, some people were saying that that was racist because they were targeting primarily Blacks.

SHEILA: (angrily) I get sick of Black people always yelling racist! That's just common sense!

Although Sheila and Jackie felt that the media focused on the negatives of the Black community, they also felt that Blacks could do something to help themselves. Issues of hypersensitivity to one's race became a source of irritation for Sheila and a few of the women I talked to. They made it clear that what was considered racism to one person was not necessarily racism to another.

As I continued to interact with the women in the shop and note the experience of being in the shop itself, I became aware of the beauty shop culture and the physical, psychological, and emotional transformations that occurred during the women's visits. This unique culture is described next.

The Miracle Worker

Sometimes called a beautician, a hair stylist, a beauty specialist, or a cosmetologist, Sheila may have been best known by her clients as the miracle worker. Women came to her shop to be repaired, often arriving incognito, wearing baseball caps and scarves to hide their hurting hair. Sheila, the miracle worker, was often thought to be able to wave a magic wand and instantly transform a mess into a masterpiece. Regardless of how poorly the women took care of their hair or how damaged their manes were, they expected Sheila to transform their appearance to that of a supermodel right off the pages of Ebony magazine.

Research has shown that advertisements for such miracles attract the attention of millions of women each year. These miracles do not apply solely to hair changes but rather to the transformation of all unacceptable appearances into something that gains social attention and acceptance. The annual profits of cosmetic and beauty companies show that women are quite generous when it comes to altering their appearances and sense of self-worth.[2]

When the hairstyles the women received did not match up to the styles and transformations they had fantasized about, their once expectant faces fell, like balloons that had just had their air let out. But the women never made a scene as a result of their disappointment. No, not in Sheila's shop. On rare occasions a few words of disappointment were said, but there were never outbursts of screaming or crying in the shop. Whether these scenes took place when the women reached home was another story. There seemed to be an unwritten rule that one could not become enemies with Sheila; after all, that would possibly mean the end of both a faithful friendship and a relationship with a competent stylist. Rather than take the risk of losing a good beautician, any disappointed patron had to deal with her feelings on her own. But when known, Sheila would work to remedy the patron's disappointment or problem.

The women trusted Sheila's abilities. According to ancient African culture, only certain people were to be trusted with the vulnerability of one's hair; it was sacred.[3] The women in the shop seemed to feel this way about Sheila. Both the beauty shop and the beautician symbolized an entity that was ordained to remedy their problems physically (hair transformation) and emotionally through pseudo-, shop-chair counseling. Maintaining good beauty shop relationships was crucial in keeping this special relationship and informal therapeutic outlet vibrant.

The women trusted Sheila over some of the Black superstitions about hair. Some common ones were "If you want your hair to grow back, only cut it when there's a full moon"; "Never cut a boy's hair before age one, or it won't grow or it will be kinky"; "If you let more than one person work on your hair at a time, your hair will fall out"; and the list goes on.[4] Considering superstitions, styles, and pseudotherapy, Sheila's job was no small matter.

The Wait

It is not uncommon for women to wait an hour or more before they begin to have their hair worked on in many larger beauty shops. This is even with a scheduled appointment. And depending on the hairstyle one is getting, a couple of hours to nearly half a day could be spent in the beauty shop. However, in Sheila's shop, most patrons had their hair worked on within twenty minutes after their arrival and were usually out of the shop within two to three hours.

Even when a patron was receiving constant attention, hours spent in the shop could seem long. So what would women do during that time? They talked! Sheila kept the shop filled with popular hair and social magazines, music, and a television, but lively discussions between the women seemed to be the most popular way of passing time.

On one occasion, I witnessed the dramatic transition of a calm conversation to a stirring one on domestic violence within minutes. The discussion got started after one woman mentioned what women should and should not tolerate in their dating and marital relationships.

SHEILA: (regarding spousal abuse) I've never been in that situation, thank God, 'cause the first time you hit me, you betta be running! Girls need to wake up! If you let the man wham you aside the head, of course he's going to do it!

JACKIE: People go as far as you allow them to go.

SHEILA: Ain't nobody gonna keep bamming [hitting] on you . . . maybe it's because my parents didn't raise me like that, and I'm strong, you know!

JACKIE: That's what my friends say about me: "Jackie, you strong." But what's hard about being strong when somebody's whamming on your behind?

SHEILA: It's like I got a cousin that used to get beat by her husband unmercifully. And she didn't grow up with that! They be thinking he gonna change.

JACKIE: You be dead by the time he change!

SHEILA: If you want my help and I get you out, and you go back, I'm through with you! 'Cause a lot of innocent people get caught in the middle.

JACKIE: And they don't think nothing about your life. So you think of yours. Think of yours! 'Cause I love Jackie! (Everyone laughs. She stands up to leave.) Well, I gotta go. See y'all.

The discussions were always interesting and, although serious, often comical. When shop talk did not involve teenage pregnancies or issues about relationships, it often turned to politics. On a different day, the women engaged in a hot debate about government officials:

SHEILA: (during the Clinton administration) Did y'all see Hilary Clinton on *Oprah*?

WOMEN: (excitedly anticipating what's next) Naw!

SHEILA: Hey, y'all, she went to talk about her book, *It Takes a Whole Village to Raise a Child*, but Oprah said, "I'd be remiss if I didn't discuss Whitewater."

WOMEN: (collectively talking) Yeah, honey! Yeah, child!

SHEILA: But they try to act like nobody else ever done nothin'. Newt probably had the cleaning people plant something [on the Clintons]. People's past is people's past!

WOMEN: (talking over each other excitedly) Yeah, that's right. Ain't no need of bringing up what happened twenty years ago!

SHEILA: I wouldn't want that office [president]. You go in one way and come out looking fifty years older!

(The television shows Hilary Clinton.)

SHEILA: They don't like her [Hilary] because she's a strong, educated woman in that good old boys network!

WOMEN: (all agree) Yeah!

SHEILA: They talkin' 'bout balancing the budget; they need to quit wasting our tax dollars on stupid stuff like this! Whitewater happened all those years ago, and they wasting all these dollars trying to see if Hilary made a little profit!

JEAN: Yeah, the whole point of investing is to gain a profit!

WOMEN: (all agree) That's right!

The women, for the most part, agreed with each other on most discussions; however, when varying viewpoints seemed to clash, great effort was made to maintain a friendly atmosphere. It was obvious when opinions were not in agreement, but the women worked hard to maintain a sense of harmony in the shop. This often occurred by way of changing the subject, stating, "We all have our views," or by trivializing and making fun of a more serious discussion. On no occasion did I ever witness any woman leaving the shop mad at another.

The Chair

At the appointed times, Sheila calls for her patrons to have a seat in her hair styling chair. The chair is symbolic of several things. First, the chair represents TLC, tender loving care. What makes this chair so special and symbolic of TLC is that women who are usually caregivers for others finally have the opportunity to be cared for. The way Sheila cares for her clients often resembles a loving mother caring for her daughter as she gently brushes her daughter's hair. This does not mean that once in the chair the treatment clients receive is an entirely gentle process. In fact, many times sitting in the chair represents pain rather than pleasure, but women are willing to endure this temporary pain to secure the attention of their listening beautician and to get the hairstyles they want.

The chair also represents the hope and possibility of being beautiful. Women willingly endure necessary pain for the sake of looking good when they leave. Although their fresh salon look often lasts for only a few hours or days, a moment of glamour or acceptance is greatly treasured. This is especially the case when a woman views herself as unattractive. This beauty transformation process can be compared to that of a caterpillar becoming a butterfly. When the women first come into the shop, they act like caterpillars; but by the time they leave, they often feel and act as if they can fly. The problem with this reaction, according to some feminist views, is that the very thing that is used by women to gain and maintain social approval is eventually turned against them and used to stereotype or degrade them.[5] An example of this backlash is a husband's expectation that his wife will keep herself up, but his complaint that she and women in general spend too much money doing so.

The third meaning the chair has is its symbolic representation of change. After a major event in a woman's life, it is not uncommon for her to dramatically change her hair. This includes cutting her hair very short, if it was once very long, or changing its color to a bold new shade. Often a woman's hair is a visual sign of new beginnings or the marking of a major event. In fact, it was during my final year of my graduate program that I let Sheila cut my hair short. This was partly out of necessity (the stress of school had left my hair in a broken condition) and partly to symbolize a new season in my life that entailed leaving the past behind.

Prices and Procedures

So what does it cost to be beautified? The answer to this question depends on how "beautiful" one wants to be. Here is a list of a variety of treatments and prices from Sheila's shop:

- Relaxer/perms: $35 and up
- Pressing: $25
- Weaves: $5 a layer
- Coloring/frosting: $25
- Cuts: $7
- Wash and set: $20
- Jheri curls: $50

I must note that Sheila's prices were much lower than those at many larger beauty shops and salons. Upon doing my own comparison, I found that some beauty shops charged at least 20 percent more than Sheila did. And Sheila's prices were generally listed for women only. Men tended to stay away from the shop, and when they did come in it was usually only to drop off someone or to pick them up. There was only one occasion in roughly two years that I witnessed a man getting his hair done in the shop. Somehow a silent rule had been established that this beauty shop was strictly a woman's domain.

I must point out the physical costs of styling treatments as well. One of the most common hair treatments that Sheila's clients received was a relaxer. Relaxers are creams containing chemicals such as sodium hydroxide (lye) or calcium hydroxide (no lye) that are used to straighten the hair. In 1947, the White-owned hair company Lustrasilk produced a hair treatment that was an early form of a relaxer, but it was not until the mid-1960s that the then-Black-owned company Johnson Products produced "Ultra Sheen Relaxer," which was chemically based and required no added heat to straighten the hair. However, even before these official relaxers, some Black men had been using a homemade version of a relaxer called "conk," short for congalene. Simple forms of congalene were often made with potatoes, eggs, and lye—which is what Malcom X was shone using in the movie *Malcom X*.[6]

Straightening the hair allows for a diversity of styles; however, the chemicals in the relaxer can cause a burning sensation on the scalp if the scalp is sensitive or the cream is left on too long. Some women experience sores on their scalps after their hair has been relaxed. In general, the longer the chemicals are left on the hair, the straighter the hair becomes. Some women who put their own relaxers on are willing to sacrifice their scalps to ensure straighter hair.

Relaxers are also known as perms in the Black community; however, the term *perm* has a different connotation for Whites. While *perm* in the Black community is usually used synonymously with *relaxer* or a way of straightening the hair, in White communities *perms* generally refer to chemical treatments used to make the hair curly.

Pressing is yet another popular hair treatment. The pressing comb was made popular by an African American woman named Madame C. J. Walker, who in 1910 was declared the first self-made female millionaire of any race. Although commonly said to be the inventor of the pressing comb, which actually was invented by the French in the 1800s, Walker did popularize the pressing comb within the African American community and the United States.[7] Pressing involves heating a metal comb in a small metal oven or on top of a stove and pulling the heated comb through the roots and ends of the hair to straighten it. The hot metal comb is primarily pulled through the roots of the hair, leaving the entire hair shaft easier to comb. Some African American women refer to the roots as "naps," "kinks," or "kitchen" (on the nape of the neck). The goal is always to have the naps, kinks, and kitchen straightened out and prevent them from "turning back" or going back·to their natural state. Many older beauticians have been known for using a heavy "grease" or hair pomade to help a press lay down straight longer.

Although deemed more healthy for the hair than chemical straighteners, the pressing comb is extremely hot. On some rare occasions, a woman may even incur a burn to her face, scalp, or ears in the process. Oftentimes African American girls undergo this type of hair treatment, because they are considered too young for chemical treatments. This process may be particularly distressing for a young girl who fears getting burned. This fear may ultimately result in a self-fulfilling prophecy. It may be the child's fear that causes her to squirm in the chair, causing the beautician actually to miss the hair and burn the skin. However, Sheila was highly skilled with the pressing comb, and I never saw her burn anyone.

Another hair styling option that some clients paid for is called a weave. Weaves do not involve chemicals or heat, and they have a different meaning for Black women than they do for White women. A weave for Black hair means adding extensions, or hair (human or synthetic), which can dramatically augment the length of the hair. This accounts for a Black woman's ability to diversify her hair styles, going from extremely short hair on one day to extremely long hair the next. Weaves for Black hair are usually sown in with a needle and special thread or knitted in with knitting needles and attached to the client's natural hair. Either can be slightly painful, due to the pulling and pressure on the head. For White women, a weave usually has to do with having color highlights added to their hair.

A fourth hair styling treatment that Sheila's clients paid for is known as a Jheri curl. Jheri curls are named after a White man, Jheri Redding, who invented a chemical process that converted straight hair to curly. In 1977, a Black man named Willie Lee Morrow came out with an adapted form of a curl for African Americans that would straighten tightly coiled hair and then curl it called the "California curl." Although the name *California curl* was popularly used, the term *Jheri curl* became synonymous with curls.[8] Jheri curls were more popular in the late 1970s and 1980s, yet several of Sheila's clients chose this styling option for its easy management. Jheri curls require processing the hair to relax it at its roots and then rolling the hair on small rods to produce a final product of naturally wavy or curly hair.

A final group of popular hair treatments is known as "freeze" styles. These hair treatments require freshly relaxed hair to be styled while wet. They require lots of setting gel and plenty of heat to harden the hair and include styles known as "candy curls," "finger waves," and "crispy French rolls." The result is a hard or "frozen" hair style that clients do not have to comb or wash for several days or weeks. Many working women choose these styles for convenience and hot weather practicalities.

These styles as well as some coloring treatments that Sheila used required the women to sit under stationary dryers for long periods. For some women, staying under the dryer resulted in heat exhaustion, hot flashes, or restlessness. In Sheila's shop it was not uncommon for women to sneak out from under the dryers both to escape the tremendous heat and to try to hear what was being said in the other room.

What were the psychological and emotional payoffs for clients who endured such rigorous treatments? A client with such a new style was often bombarded with such accolades as, "Girl, you look good!" "Oh, your husband is going to love it," or "You are going to turn some heads," from the other clients. After undergoing such treatments, the women gained an ego boost and a sense of acceptance of themselves and from others. After receiving Sheila's care, they were ready to face the world and have the world face them. Baseball caps were tucked away and scarves were put into purses. After this successful transformation, the women seemed to be indebted to Sheila for making this transformation possible and, when able, were willing to give Sheila a tip to show their appreciation.

Feminist Views

What would a feminist say about such sacrifices for "beauty"? In *Femininity and Domination*, Sandra Bartky says that psychological oppression has been institutionalized, stimulating the sexual objectification of women. By this Bartky suggests that women are fragmented and valued for their parts instead of their whole person. She states that body parts and physical appearance are separated from the rest of a woman's persona and are regarded as representatives of the total woman. The focus therefore turns from internal value to external assets.

According to Bartky, females learn early in life that they will be evaluated primarily by their appearances. Their identities and appearances are often seen as one in the same. Bartky says it is the job of the objectifier (the viewer) to make the objectified (the one being viewed) see herself as her viewer sees her. Bartky suggests that women learn to consider what others think about how they look. Whether through comments or the gestures of others, females quickly discover what is acceptable and unacceptable. After learning acceptable rules of beauty, women pass these standards on to other women, including their daughters. According to Bartky, after sufficient conditioning has taken place, a woman will learn to evaluate herself first, becoming her own worst critic. To ease her feelings of alienation, a woman begins to dictate these same standards to others. Those that rebel against stereotypical indicators of feminine beauty will find themselves ostracized. So to be socially acceptable, women have to find fault with themselves and others, as well as strive to redeem their value through costly products and services.

In *Bulletproof Diva*, author Lisa Jones addresses the fact that the sources of human hair that African Americans use for weaves and braids primarily come from Asian and European countries. This hair is collected and packaged at hair farms, sold and distributed by Caucasian and Asian men, and consumed by African American women. Jones notes that such hair product companies as Dark and Lovely, TCB, and Let's Jam are not Black-owned companies and that Black companies are not getting the bids for Black hair care. She points out one popular company, African Pride (which is White owned), has fought Black-owned companies over the use of the term *African* in their product names.[9]

In 1981, a number of Black hair companies came together in a consortium to protect their share of the market and to target their products to Black people by establishing the American Health and Beauty Aids Institute (AHBAI), which had the trademark symbol of a Black woman identified as "The Proud Lady." This would make it clear to African American customers who cared which products were Black owned and which were not. White companies began to fight back by using African American celebrities to market their products, confusing the public once again. Today, although product lines such as Soft Sheen, Pro-Line, and Revlon may advertise using African American faces, these companies have been bought out by non–African American companies.[10]

In regard to the positive factors of Black hair, Jones highlights the versatility of Black hair and points out that all hair can be manipulated to be a work of art, no matter if it is real or not. However, she also notes that some of the acid treatments that are used to destroy bacteria during the manufacturing of human hair later to be sold are not always sufficiently rinsed out, causing allergic reactions in consumers. Still another problem, she points out, is that there were no laws prohibiting the selling of dead people's hair—a situation that has been largely rectified today.

In *Hair Public, Political, Extremely Personal*, Diane Simon discusses the issue of hair discrimination and how in the workplace African Americans have been discriminated against for wearing braids, dreadlocks, and Afros.[11] However, she notes that under Title VII, Blacks' rights to wear ethnic styles are protected. She also points out that while the hair industry caters to African Americans, it does not belong to them.

In *Hair Matters*, Ingrid Banks states, "Hair is a means by which one can understand how Black women and girls view their worlds, it is essential to understand why hair matters to them [for broader cultural issues]."[12] Banks examines the politics and social control behind hair. Looking at historical data she points out how prisoners and military personnel are made to keep their hair short, as a means of control, while hippies pride themselves on wearing their hair long and reveling in that freedom and rejection of social control. She also points out that during the 1960s, the Black Afro represented Black power and pride. In addition, she reviews literature that traces the evolution of "kinky" hair as a symbol of pride in western Africa, to postenslavement, when it became a source of ridicule by Whites and internalized inferiority by slaves.[13]

In *Hair Story*, Ayana Byrd and Lori Tharps note that unkempt hair in some parts of Africa was a sign that something was wrong (e.g., death, mourning); since the head and hair were the most elevated parts of the body, hair was supposed to represent splendor and majesty, much like a crown. They further highlight the fact that there were many meanings ascribed to African and African American women's hair. They point out that in Africa hair was used to convey messages such as one's marital status, age, religion, rank, or wealth. Once Africans were brought to North America as slaves, hair was used to show humiliation, submission, and conformity. Later, hair would be used to portray artistic and creative fashion. And in the 1960s and 1970s, hair would be used to relay a political statement. Hair today for African Americans means a variety of different things, but there has been a transition to more ethnic hairstyles.

Byrd and Tharps discuss the controversy over Black women wearing their hair natural versus straight. They highlight a notable quote in 1904 by Nannie Helen Burroughs, a leader in women's issues: "What every woman who . . . straightens out [her hair] needs, is not her appearance changed but her mind changed. . . . If Negro women would use half of the time they spend on trying to get White, to get better, the race would move forward."[14] They note that while this view represents how many Afrocentric people may feel, for others, hair straightening has more to do with modernity and fashion than with being White. After all, White women have straightened their hair, too, for certain styles. And lest we assume that African American women have been the sole users of hair straighteners, African American men who have straightened their hair include Malcolm X, Nat King Cole, Little Richard, and Cab Calloway, to name just a few.[15]

Banks points out the problems and contradictions associated with straightened hair as compared to "natural" hair. She points out how for some a social activist with straightened hair is not to be taken seriously and that feminists tend to lose respect for any woman with relaxed hair. She says that hair alterations are seen as self-hatred, because processed hair greatly limits the activities of women. Such things as avoiding swimming or walks in the rain (even with an umbrella) become big deals. However, in defense of various views, Banks points out that personal choice, autonomy, and versatility are important factors as well. Finally, she notes that for some women marrying a man with "good hair" (for the sake of the children) becomes an issue, and for some men marrying a woman with long hair, seen as a symbol of femininity, becomes a major goal. Differences in the pride one takes in one's hair and hair style choices can be found between the educated and uneducated, the upper class and underclass.

Philomena Essed's (1991) concept of gendered racism can be transposed here, suggesting that the often socially inferiorized and oppressed status of women is further demoralized by the fact that women are controlled by beauty industries that are largely controlled by men—and in fact non-Black men. These industries continue to dictate to Black women, and women from all races, what is acceptable and what is not.

A Final Note

In considering feminists' views on beauty and hair and comparing them to the women who patronized Sheila's shop, it was obvious that Sheila's clients received much more than a hairdo or commercialized beauty. They also received caring friendships that went beyond a paid service and beyond the shop. If it were only socially accepted beauty that these women received in the shop, then the price they paid in time, money, and pain would be far too great. But what these women gained through support and mutual friendships could not be measured in dollar and cents. They had established a true community, and this community was located in Sheila's shop.

Notes

1. Aisha Mori, "Letting Their Hair Down," *San Gabriel Valley Weekly*, June 8, 2001, 1, 8.

2. Rita Freedman, *Beauty Bound* (Lexington, Mass.: Lexington, 1986).

3. Ayana Byrd and Lori Tharps, *Hair Story: Untangling the Roots of Black Hair in America* (New York: St. Martin's, 2001).

4. Byrd and Tharps, *Hair Story*, 24.

5. Sandra Bartky, *Femininity and Domination: Studies in the Phenomenology of Oppression* (New York: Routledge, 1990).

6. Byrd and Tharps, *Hair Story*.

7. Byrd and Tharps, *Hair Story*, 35.

8. Byrd and Tharps, *Hair Story*, 89–90.

9. Lisa Jones, *Bulletproof Diva: Tales of Race, Sex, and Hair* (New York: Doubleday, 1994).

10. Byrd and Tharps, *Hair Story*, 91–96.

11. Diane Simon, *Hair Public, Political, Extremely Personal.* (New York: St. Martin's, 2000).

12. Ingrid Banks, *Hair Matters: Beauty, Power, and Black Women's Consciousness* (New York: New York University Press, 2000), 4; also see C. R. Hallpike, "Social Hair," in *Comparative Religion: An Anthropological Approach*, ed. William Lessa and Evon Z. Vogt (New York: Harper & Row, 1972), 99–104.

13. Willie L. Morrow, *400 Years without a Comb* (San Diego, Calif.: Morrow, 1973).

14. Byrd and Tharps, *Hair Story*, 37.

15. Byrd and Tharps, *Hair Story*.

CHAPTER TWO

✂

The Realities of Being Black and Female

Personally, I'm proud to be Black and a woman! I know that when I see another Black woman, I know that this is a person that has arrived! If that person can take their head up off the pillow in the morning and walk, putting one foot in front of the other foot, and look you in the eyes, then that person has made it. When Black women walk around society, we have so many stereotypes, and we're thought of in so many different negative ways, that we have to fight just to walk around . . . we need grace to even get up in the morning because sometimes it could be depressing for us to get up, having all this over our heads. . . . It's hard, but I wouldn't choose any other way!

—A middle school teacher and beauty shop client

KIM: (referring to a TV program and an earlier conversation in the shop) Girls seem to be more responsible than boys. When you raise them, the girls seem to take more responsibility.

WOMEN: They do.

KIM: Jobs, money, saving money, keeping their money, being . . . .

WOMEN: That's true, uh-hmmm.

KIM: And boys don't. And then later on when you marry them, you gotta reteach them.

WOMEN: [laughing]

KIM: What is that about?

BURNADETTE: A lot of young men, their mothers pamper them a lot, and I know a lot of people when I was growing up, their sons weren't even allowed to do anything. I was telling them the other day of Craig . . . that's a bad habit that's picked up from his . . . daddy's side of the family; Sister Mable didn't want none of them being in the house to do anything. They didn't even fix their own plates; they sat at the table until they fixed the plate and brought the plate to them. So, see, that's something that was like passed down when they were training. I think it's all to do with training. Because now I look at my husband—my husband, he'll get in there and he'll do the same exact things that I do, sometimes more, so I think it's got a lot do with the training. If you ain't training them to be responsible and to learn how to take responsibility for things, they are not gonna have it.

WOMEN: And why they can't help sometimes?

SHEILA: That's right!

KIM: Yeah!

BURNADETTE: That's right . . . these moms . . . a lot of moms are doing their sons that way because they teach those boys to make those girls do everything.

· SHEILA: Yeah.

BURNADETTE: And those boys don't have to do anything because it's a woman's place.

KIM: Just hire a maid, huh?

MOTHER MAC: Yeah, that's what I say. Hm-mmm.

BURNADETTE: They got . . . dependent on that, because women work harder than men. A lot of them do because they don't want to be coming home and cleaning your house.

SHEILA: And some of the women don't know how to do it [clean] anyway so they [the men] better know how to do it their own self. It shouldn't just be a woman thing; it should be a man thing, too!

This chapter looks at the daily realities that working-class African American women face. The women discuss what it is like to be a Black woman in America today and the struggles Black women have. They talk about the double challenge of being both Black and female. They also discuss how Black women are different from White women, their views of welfare, and their opinions of how the media portray them.

The Experience

The gendered racism concept that Essed has shaped states that Black women are stigmatized and discriminated against on two accounts. First, they are discriminated against for being Black. Second, they are discriminated against for being women. Using salaries as a starting point, women make seventy-two cents for every dollar a man makes, with African American women earning even less than White women.[1] According to the gendered racism concept, Black women are not paranoid when it comes to their concerns about job security and equitable pay; for them, job inequities are quite real.

When asked what it is like to be a Black woman in America today, one of Sheila's clients, a former packaging worker, said:

> No, you didn't ask me that (laughs)! It's hard! . . . Everywhere you turn there's a stumbling block. They've [those in power] got something to cut you off. If you are trying to make a honest living you have a hard way to fly! If you try to work your way up to the top, you are going to drop hard back to the bottom.

This client points out the difficulty Black women have in trying to be successful. Many Black women who try to work their way to the top find resistance from supervisors and the institutions in which they work. This woman had had to leave her packaging job due to a work-related injury for which she was not responsible. This had left her feeling highly stressed and less than optimistic about her future economic condition. Many Black women with similar job instability find professional and economic conditions particularly stressful.

Berniece, a correctional officer for a women's prison, boldly voiced her frustrations with gendered racism:

> In dealing with everything, right down to the church, I don't care how you excel, how you put the words in the right place, or what kind of automobile you drive, how you excel and work like a dog, get you a fine home, because I have all this *stuff*, or how many diamonds you put on your fingers—there's always someone that's going to remind you that you're Black! And they let you know in America that Blacks have a place. Not that you're grabbing and identify. with the *place* that they say, but they let you know that you have a place being Black. As long as we're here, somebody is going to let you know that you're Black. I don't care how much money you have! That's how I feel.

Berniece, as did many of the women I interviewed, felt that her status as a Black woman remained a stigma, regardless of her accomplishments. She believed that after all was said and done, society still saw her as a minority lacking power and prestige as a result of her race and gender. Although she refused to let society's stereotypes of her hold her back, she nevertheless was aware of them. Similarly, another client who works as an office clerk stated her disappointment with employment inequities, which she contributed to racial and gender discrimination.

> There are drawbacks on everything. And me personally, I think it's a pitiful thing because I'm proud of being a Black woman. I'm very proud of that. A lot of us would like to get ahead but we don't get ahead because of race. White

people will not let a woman have a position. If a position comes along and a White and Black person are competing for that position, the White person, 99 percent of the time, will get that position. You learn to deal with that because you have to live.

This client pointed out that when race was not an issue, gender was, and when gender was not an issue, race was. In other words, Black women were constantly being judged by some standard and challenged by some obstacle. National job statistics regarding those who are financially and professionally on top seem to support this claim. Some Black women, however, believe themselves to be fortunate when it comes to their job status. Jean, one of Sheila's regular clients who had made great advances in comparison to her mother and grandmother, stated:

Well, as far as [these times are concerned,] . . . it is better than what it was when my parents were growing up. I listened to the stories even from my great-great-grandmother, and you know the situations they had to grow up in. They tell me all the time I need to count my blessings, because they really had it hard! My grandmother, she couldn't complete school because she had to work. Back then my great-grandmother had eleven children, because the more children you had, the more farmland you could have, if the children could work the land. And so that is why they had a lot of children. With my mother, being that she was the fourth child being born, she had to help raise the younger kids because there were eleven of them. She completed high school, but she wasn't able to go on to [post]secondary education, because she had to stay and help with the younger children.

Like Jean, several of the women discussed the hardships that their parents and grandparents had had to endure, counting their current challenges as minor in comparison. The women partially measured their progress by their increase in education and improved economic conditions. Although Sheila and her clients would not be considered academically and financially elite, they had definitely created better lives for themselves and their children than their families of origin, and this itself was a success.

Progress for these women was also measured by the women's perceptions of racial relations and how they were treated as Black women. The women thought racial relations were better today than in the past, because they saw Blacks as having more freedom to go and do as they pleased. However, the women pointed out areas where racial relations had not changed and could improve. Donna, a twenty-year-old single Black, stated that things were better for her than they had been for her parents, who grew up in a southern rural area. Although she had experienced some racism, she counted it as just a part of life. "You're brought up to know that people will treat you differently." She pointed to an incident when she learned her "place" in school. "A White girl, in the second grade, dropped her pencil and told me to pick it up, and without even thinking about it I picked up the pencil. I later wondered why I blindly obeyed." As she discussed this incident further, this socially conscious young African American woman came to the conclusion that the media had helped in teaching her as well as other Blacks "their places," especially as Black women. Even though Donna was my youngest interviewee, she was very much aware of social and political systems that were at work in shaping society's views, perceptions, and behaviors.

In contrast to Donna's youthful scrutiny, Miss Mary, a seventy-year-old, described what it was like to be a Black woman from her perspective.

> I would say a Black woman today, she can achieve whatever she'd like to in life, if she goes after it in the right way. She has more opportunities than Black women had a long time ago. So I think a Black woman could go just as far as she wants, if she presents herself [in the right way] and has self-esteem. She can make it.

As a person who was born during the 1920s and who had lived through several volatile decades in race relations, Mary knew that there were some barriers that Black women had to overcome, but she felt that they could overcome them even if that meant they had to work harder and deal with prejudice. This strong persevere mentality was particularly evident among several of the older clients who had made it in spite of overwhelming odds. Although Mary did not graduate from high school, she felt her life had turned out well. She based her success on the fact that she had been married for over fifty years, had raised one son who had a doctorate degree, and had given back to all kinds of people over the years.

A divorced single parent saw her heritage as an African American woman from still another perspective.

> [It is] very difficult! I'm not only Black, I'm single, and I'm in the South! I'm a single parent, and I have four children who I have worked two jobs to educate. I worked when they were small and drove back and forth to [a nearby city] to get my degree. I have been out of school ten years and still in the South. The pay is terrible . . . I mean it's really rough! To make up the difference [low pay] or to make ends meet, I am now back to working on the weekends. So it's rough and you're tired and you go [to work]. It's just rough being a single parent, but it's like double the trouble being Black and single and a single parent. It's really rough!

Being a Black woman is often complicated further if one is single and a parent. This is primarily the case when African American women find themselves in low-wage jobs and with little outside support. Statistics indicate that over two-thirds of African American children will live in a single-parent household at some point before reaching the age of eighteen. With the responsibility of a single-parent household comes added financial, emotional, and social challenges.

In her book *The Habit of Surviving*, Kesho Yvonne Scott discusses the unique challenges of Black single mothers. She points out that with the responsibility that some Black women have, including raising children on their own, it is easy for them to get into a survival mode. This mode, according to Scott, focuses on the immediate rather than the long term, allowing Black mothers to raise their children effectively, but doing little in the way of helping them to fulfill their personal and long-term goals. Instead, the focus goes to such things as "Will I be able to feed my children tomorrow?" and "Will I be able to keep a roof over my and my children's heads?" The focus shifts from thriving to mere surviving.

Gendered Racism Literature

A number of female scholars have examined the interrelationship between race and gender. Many of the following books contain experiences that closely resemble experiences of the women in Sheila's shop.

In *Everyday Racism*, Philomena Essed looks at the racial experiences of twenty-five women coming from Surinamese and African American backgrounds. In her research, Essed found that racism in the United States and in the Netherlands was based on the same foundation—an ideology of White superiority. According to her, educated and professional Whites were no less inclined to express racism than the less educated. She also found that although the women in her study experienced discrimination based on their sex, gender harassment seemed to be linked first and foremost to the fact that they were not just women but Black women.

Author Marilyn Frye points out the "double bind" that Black women face:

> One of the most characteristic and ubiquitous features of the world as experienced by oppressed people is the double bind—situations in which options are reduced to very few and all of them expose one to penalty, censure or deprivation. For example, it is a requirement upon oppressed people that we smile and be cheerful. If we comply, we signal our docility and our acquiescence in our

situation. We need not, then, be taken note of. We acquiesce in being made invisible, in our occupying no space. We participate in our own erasure. On the other hand, anything but the sunniest countenance exposes us to being perceived as mean, bitter, angry or dangerous.[2]

This double bind is applicable to women, people of color, and other groups of historically oppressed people. It should be noted that Frye's use of the concept double bind intersects with W. E. B. DuBois's concept of "double consciousness."[3] This idea of being forced to maintain two presentations of self, one that is acceptable to the dominant society and one that is real, expresses the inner warring that subordinate groups of people often feel on a daily basis.

Frye also uses a word picture, a bird cage analogy, to explain how members of a dominant group often view racial oppression as nonexistent and blame those who are in subordinate roles for limiting themselves. In her analogy, she explains that from a close and myopic view of the bird cage, one sees only one wire with a bird in the middle that could seemingly fly free; however, if one stands back and looks at the bigger picture, he or she sees several wires working in a collaborative effort to lock the bird in. This analogy closely parallels the cumulative lived experiences concept, which suggests that viewed narrowly, Black women appear to be playing the part of the victim when they imply that racism still exists, but in reality they are merely responding to and exposing years of overt and covert racism that has locked them into subjugated roles.

In her writings, Gloria Yamato notes the "internalization" of sexism and racism:

> Internalized racism is what really gets in my way as a Black woman. It influences the way I see or don't see myself, limits what I expect of myself or others like me. It results in my acceptance of mistreatment, leads me to believe that being treated with less than absolute respect, at least this once, is to be expected because I am Black, because I am not White . . . because you've been deliberately beaten down by agents of a greedy system until you swallowed the garbage. That is the internalization of racism.[4]

Yamato suggests that this internalization is the result of oppression from the dominant group that systematically mistreats the subordinate group until the subordinates begin to expect and sometimes accept oppression. This idea parallels with what Essed identifies as "inferiorizing."[5] Essed notes that White people often had low expectations for Blacks and sought to confirm these expectations through various means. This view, unfortunately, could lead to Blacks unconsciously fulfilling the expectations of Whites' inferior view of them.

In her book *Yearning*, bell hooks also confronts head on the relationship between race and sex. She examines the significance and overlap between racial and sexual hegemony. This and other writings by hooks are particularly beneficial, because hooks effectively weaves a picture of the interconnectedness of race, gender, and class. For her, "oppression in any form is oppression in every form."[6] She encourages subordinated people to confront their pain, stating that pain is a catalyst for change.

Margaret Andersen and Patricia Hill Collins point out that all people of color encounter institutional racism, but their experiences are contingent on their social class, gender, age, sexuality, and other markers of social position. Using their premise, a young, Black, working-class woman is therefore a strong candidate for institutional racism from a variety of prejudiced angles.

In *The Velvet Glove*, Mary Jackman examines the connection between race, gender, and class, and she links these concepts to their common relationship with paternalism. Jackman defines paternalism as "the principle or system of governing or controlling."[7] Paternalism involves a level of benevolence or the ability to convince others that you know what is in their best interest, according to Jackman. She points out that daily practices of discrimination do not require hostility or creating a constant state of conflict, but rather convincing subordinates that you are on their side or helping them out, thereby creating an nonconfrontational environment.

For the African American women in Sheila's shop, paternalism had been evident in job subordination, stereotypes of incompetence, and discrimination based on their gender and race. In listening to the views of the clients, I realized racial background had a bigger impact in their daily lives and experiences than gender. Although the women acknowledged that sexism and racism often went hand in hand and were both damaging, the women placed a greater emphasis on racial discrimination as being problematic than gender discrimination.

Struggles and Challenges

African American women face unique challenges as a result of a combination of racial and gender stigmas. Here, Sheila's clients discuss some of the specific challenges they face as Black women.

When asked to address her greatest challenge or struggle as an African American woman, one thirty-five-year-old, divorced client said:

> I think being a Black woman and knowing that maybe, or possibly, your adult life might be spent alone, and not with a partner, is one of our biggest struggles. That your children will get, as a role model, a mother struggling to help the children, and the effect this seems to have on them.

This possibility of remaining single with or without children is a critical concern for many Black women. Since the number of marriageable partners decreases as age increases, several of the women in Sheila's shop wondered if they would ever get married or remarried. The added challenges for a single-parent household were addressed by several of Sheila's clients who were divorced or single. Some seemed optimistic, while others were physically and emotionally drained.

Sociologist William J. Wilson explains the plight of Black single-parent families from a structuralist's point of view.[8] Wilson points out that the lack of economic stability for Black men has negative implications for Black families. According to Wilson, when a Black male is not able to support himself due to a lack of employment, he is not going to be willing to support a family. This greatly affects the number of marriageable men for Black women. Wilson goes on to say, "As the disappearance of work has become a characteristic feature of the inner-city, so too has the disappearance of the traditional married-couple family."[9] With over 50 percent of African American families being headed by a single parent, structural and economic supports for African American children are a major concern.

In *Tomorrow's Tomorrow*, Joyce Ladner recounts two important roles that African women fulfilled during slavery. One was as an economic resource to their plantation owners through both physical labor and procreation to produce new slaves. The second role was that of the matriarch. Strong bonds between mother and child were often fostered due to the absence of the father, who was often sold away from the rest of the family. Both of these patterns have continued even though circumstances have changed.[10]

Another notable challenge that the women encountered was professional hindrances. A police officer explained that her struggles were associated with proving her worth and value at work.

> Showing people that I am valuable [is my greatest struggle]. Showing them that I can do the job that I was hired to do. . . . I go through the same training that any male does, whether he's White or Black, and I don't think it should be a problem. I've had people call the station to say, "Did you send this officer?" as if I'm going to get in a uniform and dress up and pretend to be a cop. Like I want to get into their houses. [Another struggle is] showing them that I'm not just waiting to get welfare, which most of America stereotypes Black women as being. Hey, I contribute to society just as much as anybody else!

Black women are sometimes looked on by others as not being capable of doing their jobs effectively. Having their abilities and their integrity questioned is an issue with which many of these women struggle. The women in the shop wanted mainstream society to know that they, too, were resourceful, capable, and competent. They were not looking for a handout but rather a "hand up" to equal respect and opportunities.

While being questioned professionally was one struggle, being shunned and ignored was quite another. The women commented on how they sometimes had to struggle with being treated as if they were nonentities or nonexistent. An elementary school teacher stated:

> I think [my biggest struggle is] just having to understand that I am a professional and that once they [Whites] work with me and once they begin to interact with me, then they understand that I am a professional and I am very professional. I expect them to respond in a professional manner to me. But until they really start to interact with me it's "Oh, there she is" [or] "Who is she?" [They try to act like I'm not there.]

Gaining respect from White colleagues and clients was a challenge that many of these women faced. Habits for surviving that these Black women implemented at work included ignoring the fact that they were not being respected by their White colleagues, making a "scene" on their jobs, or quitting their jobs to find more respectable working relations.

Donna, Sheila's younger client, said her struggle had to do with "trying to overcome people looking at your being Black as a handicap instead of as a strength." The gendered racism concept maintains that Black women have had to continually fight against such negative social views to prevent self-inferiorization. This would be where the women actually started believing what society said about them. To prevent self-inferiorization, these Black women had to tell themselves that they were not who the media said they were. They had to regularly fight against negative stereotypes and less than civilized treatment on the part of others.

Another major challenge for many of these women was maintaining strong family ties. Specifically, the women discussed the challenges of raising positive Black children. One client stated:

> Raising children, especially Black males—to me that is a challenge! Society is not for Black males, as far as helping them to achieve in this society. . . . We're raising our children to have a mind of their own, and you always have to pray for them. To, me that is a challenge, to raise Black children in this society.

This concerned mother, who is also a nurse, sees the difficulties of raising Black children, especially Black males, in society today. The concern for young Black males, who are overrepresented in the prison system, homicide rates, and violent crimes, is a real struggle for many of these mothers.

A Black mother who is also a social worker stated:

> I can say, in the past, raising my children in a public school, they have peer pressure and all of these things around them. I've instilled within them the truth. Raising children is a lifetime load for any mother if she does it right. At the time I was raising my children, I also had to deal with jobs and education. I realized I had to have that, to go further for what I wanted. I made the determination to go back to school, because I wasn't going to mop floors all my days. I said, "Lord, I'm not going to mop floors all my days," and I went back to school. You have to have a goal . . . it was a family goal!

Having made sacrifices for their families, many of these women were accustomed to doing backbreaking work. In fact, laborious work coupled with low wages has often been the impetus for African American women seeking out educations for their children and themselves. This is to ensure that both the women and their children will have better economic futures.

Looking beyond family struggles, a juvenile detention worker discussed internal racial conflict among African American people.

> A lot of times the struggle comes from people within my own race. We have a problem, as Black people, dealing with people that might have a little more ability in one area or might come from a different background. We have a problem amongst ourselves as Black women. I don't know how to put it into words, but a lot of times as a Black woman, my biggest problem is dealing with my Black sisters.

This client was disappointed with not always being able to count on her own people for support. Conflict and competition between some Black women were areas of concern for several of the women. This matter is discussed further in the next chapter.

In addition to the previously mentioned challenges that these women mentioned, economic struggles were a central point of concern. One client bluntly stated:

> Oh, Lord! Trying to survive off of this small income [is my biggest struggle]. The average Black woman has to raise her children by herself, including myself. I was blessed because I had my mother and sister to help with my kids a lot. But when you have to pay day care, and if you're getting food stamps and you go to work, they are going to cut that off; Medicaid or AFDC [Aid to Families with Dependent Children], and you go to work, they are going to cut that off. So they are

not really helping you. You got to take the little income you make and try to take care of all of these things with it. It is hard! It really is! There's no way. I'm telling you there's just no way (laughs). The odds are really against you!

The gendered racism concept acknowledges racial and gendered oppression as the primary contributors to the feminization of poverty. Such things as unequal pay, growing single-parent households, and the economic effects of divorce on the standard of living for women and children are all variables in this cycle of poverty. Some of the women discussed their need and experiences with welfare as well as their pride in climbing out of a welfare existence. Noting the economic hardships that many of these women have faced in the past or that they are currently facing, this next section looks at their views of the welfare experience.

Women and Welfare

KIM: (based on a previous discussion) Tell me about this dollar stuff?

SHEILA: OK, we were in church one Sunday and you know, everybody was getting up and giving their little testimony about what God did and all. So this sister stood up and said, "Oh, praise the Lord, you know I just thank God, y'all, because I was worried about my rent and stuff."

BURNADETTE: Uh-hmmm.

SHEILA: "And I went down there to the office and the people that were helping me with the paperwork and all; we was talking, and you know God is good because their people helped me and now I only have to pay $2 a month rent and I . . . ."

KIM: What?

BURNADETTE: She used to pay $36 a month.

SHEILA: She used to pay $36 a month rent and they cut it down to just $2 a month.

KIM: Wow!

SHEILA: And she said, "Oh, thank you, because I didn't know how I was gonna come up with that $36." (The women all laugh at Sheila's animation.)

KIM: Uh-huh.

SHEILA: (referring to herself) Thirty-six dollars! Man, I could grab aluminum cans . . . .

WOMEN: (laughing)

BURNADETTE: And pay for the whole year! (Sarcastically) You just now praising God for $2—you should have been praising him for $36!

KIM: Really!

SHEILA: (aggravated) She was worried about the $36, y'all! You can baby-sit or anything!

BURNADETTE: Anything to make $36 to pay your rent for a month.

SHEILA: (excitedly) But let me tell you what happened; let me tell you this!

KIM: (anxiously) Uh-huh?

SHEILA: Now this is another girl I know. She only had to pay $1 a month rent—this is no lie. A dollar a month rent! Now you all know that if we didn't have rent one month, them people are getting ready to evict our butt . . . out of there, right? This girl got behind for an entire year—$1 a month!

KIM: (astonished) Really?

SHEILA: For a full twelve months! They told her if she just saved the $12, they wouldn't evict her. She didn't pay it!

KIM: Wow!

BURNADETTE: Now you're talking about ridiculous.

MS. FOSTER: That is a fool.

BURNADETTE: Isn't that stupid?

SHEILA: Hold up . . . $12 for the year?

KIM: Uh-huh.

WOMEN: (laughing)

SHEILA: It's happening in America!

BURNADETTE: And all of us hardworking people barely can scrape by and pay our $450 a month rent; we praying hard for that money and they don't have to pay but a dollar a month. I'm sorry, but I can't have no sympathy on somebody who only pays $1 a month [rent]!

The women told me stories of people they knew who had "gotten over" on the system, but those who had been in the system and had actually experienced it themselves told a very different story. When the women talked about their use of government assistance, they used the term *welfare* to refer to the federal program known as Temporary Assistance to Needy Families (TANF), formerly known as Aid to Families with Dependent Children (AFDC). These women had identified themselves as receiving a monthly cash allowance along with medical care benefits and food stamps. Out of the seven women who had previously received welfare, three received assistance for less than a year. These three women used federal aid to help stabilize their families during transitional periods and were working soon after their temporary time on welfare. Three other women legally worked consistently while receiving minimal assistance, using their benefits to subsidize employment wages and pay for child care. And one woman used welfare opportunities to help her receive a bachelor's degree and secure full-time employment.

This contradicts the media's image of Black women who receive welfare as being lazy, lifeless women who idly wait to receive a dole. These women all worked toward a goal while receiving assistance and worked hard to get out of the welfare system and quickly gain financial independence by finding full-time jobs with benefits. Each of the women stated that welfare was not and should not be used as a long-term means of maintaining a livelihood. Berniece, who formerly received welfare, stated that TANF was useful in helping some women break free of abusive situations.

> I don't downgrade welfare for those ladies that need it. I would rather see them get a check, and some food stamps, and feed those children, than to see them out there in the street begging for bread! But when you have a lady that will just stay on welfare, and figure that welfare is enough for them, I don't buy it! I don't go along with that. And I feel like if you're just going to have babies just to get a check, I don't go along with that! I believe that welfare should be for those people that really need it.

Berniece first started receiving welfare after an abusive former husband refused to allow her to work but would not support her and the children. Even though she was put into a position where she needed assistance, she worked hard to get off welfare and earned an associate's degree, which enabled her to work in the prison system. And although she criticized the practice of some women staying on welfare for extended amounts of time or having additional children to receive larger checks, under the 1996 welfare reform laws these options are no longer possible.

With the high cost of child care, another client stated that her reason for being on welfare in the past was to offset day care cost.

> I don't feel bad about being on the welfare system for a while. But I had a motive. I wasn't going to be on welfare all of my life. I decided this is not how I want to raise my kids. I was just on it long enough to do better. And once God helped me to get a better job, I was able to get off of it.

This woman did not see welfare as a way of life or the ideal situation in which to raise her children. Instead, welfare was strictly a means to an end for a brief period in her life. This was reiterated by other clients who received assistance.

Policymakers have long since abandoned the idea of helping the poor improve their economic situations and have instead focused on reducing welfare dependency.[11] Americans generally stereotype the majority of those they believe to be on welfare as poor urban Black women, and TANF is generally thought of as the sole "welfare" program in existence. In reality, TANF is only a small part of what is considered welfare, and Black women do not make up the majority of those receiving it.[12]

Recent debates regarding welfare and its uses and misuses have brought negative images of women on welfare to the forefront. The underlying belief about women who receive welfare has been that these women are looking for a free ride at the expense of the American taxpayer.[13] Afraid that handouts will encourage dependency, programs such as TANF inadvertently stigmatize those who receive assistance to minimize the likelihood that recipients will get too comfortable and to make a statement to onlookers that aid comes at a high emotional price.[14] Although money is often cited as the catalyst for this type of treatment, American values such as financial independence, self-sufficiency, and hard work are at the heart of welfare hostilities.[15]

Although many people seem to believe that choosing to receive assistance is an easy option, one client who is a schoolteacher highlighted the stigma associated with receiving welfare:

> I didn't have a job, because something happened to my other job. . . . I didn't want to go back home [to her mother's]. To my mom, it [being on welfare] was always like taboo! I don't know why. . . . She wouldn't allow it. She said, "You had this baby and you are going to take care of this baby." . . . Then I got the job and I didn't need the assistance.

Poverty is often explained and categorized in one of three ways: individualistic, structural, and fatalistic.[16] *Individualistic* reasons put the responsibility of poverty on the individual. It assumes that people receive what they deserve, and if one works hard enough, upward mobility is attainable. *Structural* reasons focus on social systems that are economically and socially oppressive, therefore causing poverty. Things such as the lack of jobs or classism are identified as the reasons for poverty. Finally, *fatalistic* reasons suggest that uncontrollable, nonsystematic factors such as illness or bad luck lead to poverty. Poverty is seen more as an outcome of fate or related to factors that are outside of one's control. This view is confirmed in a study conducted by Mark Rank in which fifty families that received welfare were interviewed. The majority of respondents in Rank's study believed that they had little control over immediate circumstances that required them to receive welfare.[17]

When I asked one client whether she had ever received welfare and the reason why she needed it, she stated:

> Well, once, but not too long a period of time. But that was when I was expecting my baby, and I had to get on AFDC in order to pay the bills. So I maybe stayed on that until six months after she was born. Until they paid all of the hospital bills, and then I came off.

In a study done by Karen Seccombe and colleagues, the lack of medical in-surance was found to be a major catalyst for many women seeking govern-ment assistance.[18] Even when a woman had regular employment, if she had children but did not have health care benefits, she was likely to need outside assistance to help cover expensive medical costs.

Examining the psychological effects of being on welfare, Nancy Goodban interviewed 100 Black single mothers on AFDC. The purpose of the study was to understand how these women viewed themselves on welfare and to identify coping strategies for being on welfare. Once again the women viewed their situations as atypical and the result of uncontrollable forces. Most of the respondents saw themselves as being on welfare for a temporary span of time. Goodban found that 61 percent of the women interviewed felt some sense of shame at various times for being on welfare. Those that had in-ternalized the social ideologies and beliefs in the American dream were most likely to blame themselves for their situations. Those coming from a lower social class were more likely to have their self-esteem affected by the stigma of their welfare status. Those women coming from higher economic classes felt less stigmatized, even though they still blamed themselves and their lack of effort for being on welfare. This latter group felt less stigma, because they felt that their welfare status was temporary.[19]

One client, who previously received welfare but is now a schoolteacher, discussed how she managed to distance herself from the stigma of welfare and trained herself not to become dependent on welfare checks.

> I was on it, but I wasn't on it in a sense, whereas I didn't rely on it. You know how you're supposed to cash your checks on the first of the month? Well, I was defiant. I would try to live without doing that, so I would not run to the post office or the mail box to get it. Certain habits people have, you always see them in the stores on the first of the month, but it would not be me. I would refuse to let it swallow me up, and I would not be dependent upon it.

The tenacity with which this woman and others refused to accept welfare as a way of life was commendable and courageous. They wanted better. Emo-tionally and behaviorally distancing themselves from many of the habits that they associated with dependency, these women overwhelming convinced me that welfare was not a way of life for them.

A similar finding was noted by Liane Davis and Jan Hagen, who examined how women receiving AFDC dealt with the stigma of being on welfare. They interviewed sixteen women, ranging from teen mothers to middle-aged mothers. Their study found that none of the women liked being on welfare. All of the women thought that it was degrading and wanted to get off welfare as soon as possible. Older women felt especially demeaned by being on welfare. This shame often justified silence when it came to letting their children know that they were receiving aid. While the women agreed that some teenage mothers may want to have babies to receive checks, they all agreed that this was not their case. Most of the women in the Davis and Hagen study rejected the stereotype that women on AFDC in general bore children to receive aid or to increase their welfare checks. However, some women thought welfare should not increase if a woman had additional children while receiving public assistance.[20]

In summation, the clients I interviewed who at one time needed welfare assistance worked hard to get off welfare as soon as possible. Out of the seven who received assistance, five were off within two years. A welfare existence was not something that the women desired for themselves or their children. As for the thirteen women in my study who had not received public assistance, they generally felt that assistance was useful for those who temporarily needed it but thought that it should not be used for long-term purposes.

Media Images

Karl Marx proposed that those who controlled the means of production also controlled the production of ideas.[21] Various authors have argued that those who control the media have historically stereotyped Black women as Aunt Jemimas—the nurturing caregiver types—or as Jezebels—sexually promiscuous deviants.[22] These two opposing images can be traced back to slavery, when some slaves took on domestic duties, such as caring for the master's children, while others were said to have hypnotized him with their rhythmic movements and "animalistic" sexuality, causing him to commit and excusing him from sexual exploitation.[23] At times, these two unsolicited roles were carried out by the same woman.

The media, particularly music videos, have been criticized by some as reducing the totality of womanhood to mere body parts. When asked about their perceptions of how the media portrayed Black women, the women in the shop discussed this dichotomy. They overwhelmingly saw themselves differently from the common negative media images. One client had this to say about Black women and the media:

> They try to portray Black women as being ignorant, and uneducated, and basically the stereotypes of Aunt Jemimas, and we're not. We're educated women, and hard workers, and basically we can provide for ourselves. We don't need anyone to take care of us. But we all desire to have a mate in life, but

that's not saying we want anybody to take care of us. But society makes everybody else see us as poor people, uneducated people, stupid people, and always doing housekeeping.

Like this woman, each of the women identified herself as an intelligent, hardworking, independent, and moral individual. Demeaning media images were seen as a strike against womankind in general and Black women in particular. Another client stated:

> I think most of us are portrayed as people that are heard but not seen. I really do think that anything negative in our society is associated with us. Initially when I heard of AIDS, I heard that the Whites were the AIDS carriers. When they're talking about killing and stealing, and the person involved is Caucasian or some other race, some way they will show a minority. Maybe in the background, but they will show a minority somewhere in an effort to associate us with all the negative aspects in our society. So I think that the media has really done a disservice to our race.

Many of the women believed that the media played a big part in labeling African Americans as deviants. As this woman noted, even when a social problem did not directly involve Blacks, the media usually found some way to include at least one Black face in the picture. This phenomenon was discussed in *White Racism*, where Joe Feagin and Hernan Vera identify the role of the media in perpetuating negative racial stereotypes. They cite how a former president made use of television time to heighten paranoia of Black on White crimes, to win electoral votes.[24] Although Whites are more likely to be killed by other Whites and African Americans by other African Americans, stereotypical media images such as this only serve to reinforce negative views of African American people among the general population. In addressing racial inequities, Derrick Bell states:

> Modern discrimination is, moreover, not practiced indiscriminately. Whites, ready and willing to applaud, even idolize Black athletes and entertainers, refuse to hire, or balk at working with, Blacks. Whites who number individual Blacks among their closest friends approve, or do not oppose, practices that bar selling or renting homes or apartments in their neighborhoods to Blacks they don't know.[25]

Bell makes it clear that positive media images of Blacks did not translate into equitable treatment in the larger society. While Blacks are often praised for their talents in one setting, they are still scorned for their color in others.

A client discussed the subtleties of magazine layouts and how Blacks were portrayed in them.

> They're changing [media images]. For years while I was growing up, we were always on the left, and we were always turned downward or looking at a person directly ahead. We are never in the center of a magazine. We're usually off to the side. And they have us always looking up to a White person, or looking down admiring a White person. There's always some little game that the media plays. You notice patterns, when you have as many magazine subscriptions as I have.

This client made a mental note of the subordinate angles in which African Americans were placed in photo layouts. She pointed out that Blacks were often looking up to a White counterpart or off to the side in an inconspicuous manner. After listening to her comments and examining magazine layouts, I found her comments to be validated in several cases.

Even though there were many negatives mentioned by the women, a few women pointed out some positive changes in the roles of African American women. They commented on the increase in strong Black female characters on television. Seeing women such as Claire Huxtable from the former television program *The Cosby Show*, which depicted Mrs. Huxtable as an intelligent and professional family woman, made these women proud. However, as a whole, the women thought that the media did more harm than good as it related to Black female images.

Popular journalist Lisa Jones has raised the issue of the lack of positive Black female images and Black heroines. Citing the 1975 movie *Mahogany* with Diana Ross, she notes the need for more strong Black heroines while pointing out how the media and movies sometimes subtly tell Black women that if they are strong and successful, they will end up without a man or lose their Blackness altogether.

Finally, when it came to beauty standards and other comparisons to White women, many of Sheila's clients blamed the media for adopting myopic views of beauty. They felt that media views usually pointed to White features as being most desirable. The women discuss this more in depth in the next section, when looking at the similarities and differences between Black women and White women.

Black Women versus White Women

Essed suggests that Black women are often put at odds with White women.[26] Although these two groups share a common gender, the difference in race is often seen as a barrier between the two. In answering the question of whether there is a difference between Black women and White women when it comes to beauty, and considering differences between Black and White women, a retired Black woman stated:

> I don't think that they look no better than we do. I don't think that they can do any better than we do, but there is one thing a lot of colored women [do]. They let their self-esteem get low. . . . So I think that the Black woman should keep her self-esteem real high and go after what she wants in life. There's no difference between her and the White woman, only the color of her skin.

This woman believed that Black women were just as beautiful and talented as White women; however, Black women needed to work on their self-esteem. Although this client stated her point very matter-of-factly, centuries of negative views of Black beauty have had an effect. Even after Black beauty has become more celebrated and accepted, the ability of some African Americans to break free of internalized self-hatred has proved laborious. Countering these negative self-images, Sheila's sister Sassy stated, "Black women are beautiful! They are an asset to society. Black women are smart, educated women that work hard. They make good mothers. If there are any eligible Black men out there, find a Black woman!"

The major physical differences between Black and White women that the women pointed out had to do with hair and skin color. While some clients joked about wishing it was as easy to care for their hair as they perceived it to be for White women, they commented on their pride and appreciation of their own unique beauty, diversity in skin tones, and plethora of hair types. This being said, since slavery, many Black women with lighter complexions and long or straighter hair have experienced certain privileges that their darker sisters have not (this point also applies to Black men).

In America, African features, dark skin color, and the tightly coiled hair that protected African scalps from the scorching sun were deemed unattractive and inferior by the Europeans. Blacks who were lighter or who more closely resembled Whites (due to involuntary racial mixing) were often treated better and given house jobs instead of field work. After the abolishment of slavery, lighter skin and loosely curled hair or "good hair" translated into social assets and advantage.[27] Today, although slavery is officially over, lighter-skinned African American women unfortunately still often hold a certain unspoken higher spot in the pecking order over darker African American women due to a social obsession with color and colorism.

Several of the women pointed out what they saw as other differences. A juvenile correctional worker stated:

To me White women have more of an opportunity in the workforce. A lot of times it's because of who they know. Society has a tendency to just automatically assume that a Caucasian will do a better job or that a Caucasian is more trustworthy. So whether that person is qualified or not, they will get the job and be helped along the way.

This belief that White women were still privileged when it came to jobs was echoed among the women. One of Sheila's older clients who was no longer working stated:

Well, things a White women does, a Black woman wouldn't attempt to do. Number one, Black women can deal with stress better than a White woman. And a Black woman can deal with hardships better than a White woman, because we came up the hard way. They came up the easy way. So when things get tough, we can always work it out without suicide or killing our kids, or whatever, you know. We always work our problems out.

In the shop, the image of the strong Black woman who could handle any difficulty or hardship was reiterated by several clients. Ironically, it was this same superwoman image that was also seen as a burden or "habit" that many of these same women wanted to shake. In one sense, the women took pride in their emotional, physical, and mental strength, but on the other hand, it was their strength that made many of these women feel like machines rather than human beings. According to Joyce Ladner, "All dominant people must necessarily be strong, but all strong people are not necessarily dominant."[28] She points out that Black women are romanticized for their almost superhuman strength yet criticized for it, too. However, as she notes, just because Black women are strong does not mean they are domineering.

In her book *When Chickenheads Come Home to Roost*, Joan Morgan dispels the idea of the "Strongblackwoman—SBW" largely because it is equated with the "Blacksuperwoman—BSW" who is supposed to be able to handle any crisis, devoid of her need for love, attention, or companionship. She suggests that the myth of the SBW was originally started by Whites to justify their less than womanly treatment of Black women. Morgan asks why, if Black women are so strong, that they are more likely to die than White women from cancer, strokes, AIDS, and heart disease. Instead, Morgan suggests that Black women are strong, Black, and women but not Blacksuperwomen. Black women feel, have needs, and hurt like anybody else.[29]

In *Divided Sisters*, Midge Wilson and Kathy Russell point out several tensions that exist between the two races of women. They discuss the competition among the two groups of women over scholarships, promotions, and men. When a White woman dates or marries a Black man, they point out, many Black women see it as stealing their men.[30] This point of contention is especially magnified when looking at 2002 census data that indicate that only 48 percent of Black families were married-couple families, while 43 percent were maintained by Black women with no spouse present. In comparison, 82 percent of White families were married-couple families, and only 13 percent were headed by White women with no spouse present.[31]

These authors also state that Black women are more equal to their Black male partners, because the women work as hard as the men, dating back to slavery, and that the income of the Black mother is still needed today. The necessity for Black women to work to help support their families results in the elevated status of Black mothers and more equity in power within Black homes. With differing circumstances, Russell and Wilson see White marriages as being more unequal in power. Some of the other differences between Black and White women that the authors note are as follows:

- Black little girls are told to stay out of the sun; White little girls are encouraged to play in the sun.
- Black girls are given White dolls to play with; White girls are not given Black dolls to play with.
- Black girls are allowed to play with White girls, but not the reverse.
- Black women tend to age gracefully due to melanin; White women age less gracefully.
- White women may have bad hair days; Black women have "bad hair."
- White women have never experienced sitting and having their mothers pull their heads or pop them in the head for moving as their mothers tried to tame their hair with grease, lotion, water, and a thousand rubber bands.
- White women don't have to worry if their hair gets wet or about rolling it at night.
- The majority of White women shave their legs; this is not necessarily the case with Black women.
- Voluptuous Black women are accepted more than voluptuous White women.
- Abortion is not as readily accepted by Black women as by White women; motherhood is a prized role in the Black community.
- Black women are less likely to commit suicide than White women.
- Most Black women have had to work even after marriage; many White women had options.

- By age thirty, three-fourths of all White women are married; fewer than half of Black women are married by this age.
- White women discipline their kids with reason; Black women use strong words or physical force.
- White women have experienced gender discrimination; Black women have experienced race, class, and gender discrimination.
- White women have headed the feminist movement; Black women have been subjugated by White feminists.
- Black women are domestics; White women are employers.[32]

In fairness to White women, Wilson and Russell acknowledge that White women did not have it easy in the early days of American history, either. They discuss how White women were relocated to a new land, had to work the land, and had to deal with their husbands' sexual improprieties toward African women. Much could be said about the injustices that White women and women in general have suffered irrespective of color.

Finally, in support of gender solidarity, some of Sheila's clients stated that they did not see substantial differences between Black and White women. A county clerk said, "I don't think there is any difference. I really don't. Their thinking may be different. It is different from ours, I think, because of our culture. But coming right down to it, being women, I don't think there is a difference." Although the women discussed both physical and cultural differences between Black and White women, the shared gender struggle seemed to bridge some of the gap between the two.

One Word

To summarize what it is like to be a working-class African American woman in America today, I asked Sheila's clients to describe their experiences in one word or phrase. Collectively, they described both the positives and the negatives. One client stated:

> It's a *trial*, because every day when you wake up and go out, you don't know who you will come in contact with. It's maybe someone who's going to treat you fairly, and that is all we ask anyway is to be treated fairly. You may meet someone who has a preconceived notion about you. They are going to treat you that way. You have to figure out how you are going to act to them. There are times that you want to lash back, but if you lash back every time, sooner or later you will land up in jail. It makes you a little angry. It's a *trial* because you don't know how you will have to react that day. I may be wrong saying this, but I don't know because I have never been White living in America. But Whites go and act the

way they want to that day on their job and they can come in with their emo-
tions on end. They can come in feeling however they want to, but I have always
felt that if I went on a job and I did what I felt like doing that day I would be
fired. So I say it is a *trial*, because they can come in, in their testy way, and I have
to put up with it, but I can come in my testy way and I better just try to keep it
under control. It's a *trial* every day, and not just you—you don't know what your
family members are going to go through that day, and then they come back and
report to you what happened and you have to keep it under control!

For this woman, being an African American woman in America was a trial.
She voiced her anguish and anger at living from day to day not sure how she
would be treated by others, simply because of her race and gender. For her, being Black meant having to decide how to act ahead of time and not reacting vi-
olently sometimes when she felt like it. It also meant feeling powerless at times.
    Another client came to a similar conclusion:

Struggle (laughs)! The reason I say *struggle* is because I'm a single mother trying to pay for a house, support a child, and work ten-hour days. You got to
come home and cook, and you got HRS [a social service agency] breathing
down your back if you don't take care of these kids. It's a *struggle* from one day
to another. . . . You constantly *struggle* to be a good mother. You *struggle* to stay
up to par at the top of your job. And you *struggle* to be accepted by society, as
a Black woman, because, quote, you're not beautiful and you're nothing. So
you're *struggling* to be accepted and loved and you're *struggling* just to be a part
of society. And when people keep putting their feet on you, you have to *struggle* just to keep from going under!

For this client, it was a struggle professionally, personally, mentally, financially, and socially to be a Black woman. According to her, Black women
have to overcome challenges at every level to survive.
    A client who is currently employed as a maid said:

Trouble! You basically go from one obstacle to another. Sometimes it's like one obstacle to another. It makes you feel good when you can stand and come out on top.
A lot of people just let them just kick them and don't get up. They just stay down
instead of saying, "Oh, that's all you got," and get back up. I have learned not to
just lay there and take it and feel sorry for myself. I got pregnant at an early age,
but I was determined to finish school and I did! I walked and found my first job.

Although she faced challenges and trouble as a Black woman, this client had
a determination to overcome any obstacle rather than feel sorry for herself.
This quality was evident in most of the women's lives.

Sheila's vocal client Berniece saw the plight of being Black and female in a more favorable way. "*Blessed,* because the Scripture says that the first shall be last and the last shall be first." The general belief that one day God would justify and make wrongs into rights resonated with several of the women. A secretary also focused on the positives. "*A great experience!* I'm proud to be an African American woman in America today!" Finally, a client who was a packaging worker stated, "*Proud!* I'm proud to be an African American woman today, even with the struggles I have. You can't pity yourself, [saying,] 'Because I'm Black, nobody likes me'—all of that. Where there's a will there's a way. You can be and do whatever you want to."

Even though there were unique challenges for these women, none of the women had any regrets or apologies regarding being Black or a woman. More than ever they were determined to succeed and to enjoy their lives.

Theoretical Conclusions

The three racial relations theories discussed in the introduction were each applicable to various parts of this chapter. Each one offers a particular insight into who these women are. First, when looking at what it is like to be an African American woman, the cumulative lived experiences perspective is useful in acknowledging that the women in Sheila's shop face daily acts of racism and discrimination. Images of Black women constantly being shown in connection with promiscuity or welfare were regular realities for working-class African American women. They also had to deal with having their authority and competence challenged in working and social environments. The cumulative lived experiences concept points out that these sporadic daily battles with racist ideologies are not within themselves grounds for the women to be angry. Instead, it is the cumulative effect of years of racist practices that eventually leads to outrage and separation from those associated with racial hegemony.

Second, the gendered racism concept offers us insights into how the women deal with the double bind of racial and gendered oppression, suggesting that Black women have to deal with both types of oppression. It also helps us to understand how the women perceived issues of discrimination on their jobs. Some of the women felt that they were treated with less respect on their jobs due to their double minority status. The women also felt that when it came to colleague respect and job promotions, they were at times left out all together.

In addition to lending employment insights, the gendered racism concept highlights the fact that Black women are often alienated from both Black men and White women. This is because Black women are at times put at odds with Black men over gender inequalities and then made to feel defensive toward White women over racial differences, job promotion opportunities, and White women's relationships with Black men.

Finally, the habit of surviving concept is helpful when looking at the challenges and struggles that Sheila's clients faced. The women's concerns about their children and families, overcoming negative stereotypes, and dealing with financial difficulties caused many of these women to engage in what Scott refers to as a warrior mode. This habit of surviving often caused the women to prepare for the worst and to expect problems. It also made it difficult for them to break free of the superwoman image, which was seen as a virtue as well as a curse. On the one hand, Black women liked being portrayed as pillars of strength, yet, on the other hand, this very virtue seemingly suggested that Black women needed no one and could single-handedly deal with anything, leaving them isolated from support and feeling alone.

In the next chapter, the women discuss the issue of Black families and communities. They highlight the importance of their families as well as some of the critical problems facing their families and communities.

Notes

1. U.S. Census Bureau, *Current Population Reports: Money Income in the United States: 1999* (Washington, D.C.: U.S. Government Printing Office, 2000).

2. Marilyn Frye, *The Politics of Reality* (Trumansburg, N.Y.: Crossing, 1983,) 5.

3. W.E.B. DuBois, *The Souls of Black Folk* (New York: Fawcett, 1961).

4. Gloria Yamato, "Something about the Subject Makes It Hard to Name," in *Changing Our Power: An Introduction to Women's Studies*, ed. Jo Whitehorse Cochran, Donna Langston, and Carolyn Woodward (Dubuque, Iowa: Kendall-Hunt, 1988), 72.

5. Philomena Essed, *Everyday Racism* (Claremont, Calif.: Hunter House, 1990), and *Understanding Everyday Racism* (Newbury Park, Calif.: Sage 1991).

6. bell hooks, *Yearning: Race Gender, and Cultural Politics* (Boston: South End, 1990).

7. Mary Jackman, *The Velvet Glove* (Berkeley: University of California Press, 1994), 9.

8. William J. Wilson, *The Truly Disadvantaged* (Chicago: University of Chicago Press, 1987), and *When Work Disappears: The World of the New Urban Poor* (New York: Knopf, 1996).

9. Wilson, *When Work Disappears*, 87.

10. Joyce A. Ladner, *Tomorrow's Tomorrow: The Black Woman* (Garden City, N.Y.: Doubleday, 1971).

11. Jared Bernstein, "Rethinking Welfare Reform," *Dissent* 40 (Summer 1993):277–79; Janet Poppendieck, *Sweet Charity* (New York: Viking, 1998).

12. Howard J. Karger and David Stoesz, *American Social Welfare Policy: A Pluralist Approach*, 3d ed. (New York: Longman, 1998).

13. Liane Davis and Jan Hagen, "Stereotypes and Stigma: What's Changed for Welfare Mothers," *Affilia* 11 (1996): 319–37.

14. Nancy Goodban, "The Psychological Impact of Being on Welfare," *Social Service Review* 59 (1985): 403–22.

15. Bob Herbert, "The Real Welfare Cheats," *New York Times*, April 26, 1996; Poppendieck, *Sweet Charity*.

16. Goodban, "The Psychological Impact"; also see Karen Seccombe, Delores James, and Kimberly Battle-Walters, "They Think You Ain't Much of Nothing: The Social Construction of the Welfare Mother," *Journal of Marriage and the Family* 60 (1998): 849–65.

17. Mark Rank, *Living on the Edge: The Realities of Welfare in America* (New York: Columbia University Press, 1994).

18. Seccombe, James, and Battle-Walters, "They Think You Ain't Much of Nothing."

19. Goodban, "The Psychological Impact."

20. Davis and Hagen, "Stereotypes and Stigma."

21. Karl Marx and Friedrich Engels, *The German Ideology* (New York: Lawrence & Wishart, 1970); see also K. Sue Jewell, *From Mammy to Miss America and Beyond: Cultural Images and the Shaping of U.S. Social Policy* (New York: Routledge, 1993), 18.

22. Jewell, *From Mammy to Miss America.*

23. Midge Wilson and Kathy Russell, *Divided Sisters: Bridging the Gap between Black Women and White Women* (New York: Doubleday, 1996), 113.

24. Joe R. Feagin and Herman Vera, *White Racism: The Basics* (New York: Routledge, 1995).

25. Derrick Bell, *Faces at the Bottom of the Well* (New York: Basic Books, 1992), 6.

26. Essed, *Everyday Racism.*

27. Ayana Byrd and Lori Tharps, *Hair Story: Untangling the Roots of Black Hair in America* (New York: St. Martin's, 2001), 14–17.

28. Ladner, *Tomorrow's Tomorrow*;35.

29. Joan Morgan, *When Chickenheads Come Home to Roost: My Life as a Hip Hop Feminist* (New York: Simon and Schuster, 1999).

30. Wilson and Russell, *Divided Sisters.*

31. Jesse McKinnon, *The Black Population in the United States: March 2002*, Current Population Reports, Series P20–541 (Washington, D.C.: U.S. Census Bureau, 2003).

32. Wilson and Russell, *Divided Sisters.*

CHAPTER THREE

✂

African American Families and Communities

Many books have been written about the Black community but very few have really dealt with the intricate lives of the people who live there.

—Joyce Ladner, *Tomorrow's Tomorrow*

BURNADETTE: My mama never showed me how to cook, because my dad never wanted us in the kitchen and my mama in kitchen, so she never showed us how to cook, so when I got out and when I got married, I had to try and figure it out [laughing].

WOMEN: Yeah.

BURNADETTE: Yeah, my daddy would only eat my mama's cooking; some daddies are like that . . . .

WOMEN: Wow!

MOTHER MAC: No, that's sad.

WOMEN: [laughing]

KIM: Whoa! But you know I know people like that, like a friend of ours; the mom, she's a caterer and she's a great cook, but her daughter can't cook because the mother's always catering, always cooking, and so she doesn't cook.

BURNADETTE: It was so funny, I remember one time when I had become an adult and I went to my mom's house, we were getting ready for Christmas or something.

KIM: Uh-huh.

BURNADETTE: And my mama would say, "OK, Burnadette, you peel the potatoes." Well, mind you, she had never showed me how; I was really annoyed at this time, and she said, "OK," . . . and I said, "How?" and she looked at me like, What do you mean how . . . you asking me how? I'm like "You've never showed me!"

KIM: That's right.

BURNADETTE: She said, "Oh, Burnadette, that's an easy thing," and I said, "No, you've never showed me how to peel a potato so how am I'm gonna learn (with an attitude). I'm gonna just walk in the kitchen and know knowledge on how to peel a potato." She was out done with me, but I'm like, "You've never showed me. Don't get mad with me—get mad at yourself!"

In this chapter, the women openly discuss the status of African American families. They point out the strengths and weaknesses of Black communities, as well as some of the biggest threats in their communities today. They discuss relationships between Black men and women, candidly talking about who has it hardest between African American males and females.

Families

I would like to see more mother-and-father families. It took two of them to make a child, it will take two of them to raise a child. That is not to say that a single mother can't try, but it is difficult, and I think they [Black women] are under pressure. But again I think that we are family oriented. Sometimes Grandma can be there to pick up the pieces, but a mother cannot teach a boy how to be a man, and a man can't teach a girl how to be a woman.

—An elementary school teacher and beauty shop client

Several factors have affected the status of Black families. First, the marriage gradient, which looks at the number of available single women in proportion to the number of available single men, indicates a numerical imbalance among African Americans. According to 2000 Census data, there were approximately 8 percent more African American women than men among those fifteen years of age or older, creating a nearly two million-person gap between African American women and men among this segment of the population. The percentage gap grows larger when one specifically compares the number of never-married women to men ages twenty-five and older.[1]

Marriage rates for Black women are said to be positively correlated with levels of education. In his research, sociologist William J. Wilson suggests that Black women who are better educated are more likely to marry than Black women with little or no education.[2] However, the percentage of married African Americans dropped from 64 percent in 1971 to 48 percent in 2002.[3] This decline in marriage rates for African Americans is not based solely on a lack of commitment on the part of Blacks to marriage, because marriage rates have declined in general over the last several decades. However, this number does partly reflect several social and structural problems that have directly affected Black males and Black communities, including high unemployment rates, premature deaths, high homicide rates, poor health care access, HIV/AIDS, and an increase in criminal convictions and confinement.[4]

One of the direct implications of having fewer single marriageable Black men is having more nonmarried Black women and an increase in single Black female parent households. The overall number of children growing up in single-parent households has risen across racial and ethnic lines, yet the number of Black children being raised in single female-headed households is well above 50 percent. In the absence of available marriageable Black men, the women noted that heterosexual Black women who wanted families were left with the decision to do without marriage and children altogether, raise children alone, or marry a person of another race.

As we discussed the state of Black families and Black communities in Sheila's shop, many of the women talked about the need for stronger nuclear family ties. The women emphasized the need for both parents to be present but also noted their ability to do all of the parenting themselves, if necessary. One recently married mother stated:

> Today I feel that a lot of young [Black] women are seeking out mates, because they don't want to be the typical [stereotype] with people saying, "All [Black] females want to do is have babies and live on welfare." If you really ask the young Black female, she would say, "I want what everybody else has. I would like to have a husband, to have children, and live in a nice home."

This woman believed that Black women are no different from any other woman. They aspired to two-parent families, too. However, while most of the women hoped to have a two-parent family, decreased numbers of marriageable Black men coupled with a warrior mode mentality (one of the habits of surviving) often caused these women to settle for the families that they had rather than look toward structural changes and a different future.

Sheila described the status of Black families in this way:

> [It is] very sad. It is pitiful to see so many single mothers and to see so many fathers that got kids everywhere, and that is terrible. . . . A lot of people are going to disagree with me, but I think we need to get back to mommy and daddy. . . . I don't care how much they try to say we can love this child the same, you need that mom and that dad in that home with the kids.

Traditional values regarding the family were quite evident. Overall, the women in Sheila's shop held strongly to the ideal of two-parent heterosexual families,[5] even though many of them had experienced single parenting at one point or another.

Another factor that affects the status of Black families is the divorce rate. African Americans overall have a higher divorce rate than Whites and other ethnic groups.[6] This higher divorce rate among African Americans is largely explained by the socioeconomic status of many Blacks. Poor socioeconomic conditions, based on unemployment, low income, or little education, all contribute to higher divorce rates for Blacks and other racial and ethnic groups. Research suggests that the lower the socioeconomic status, the more likely one is to divorce.[7] As the income levels of Blacks increase, their divorce rates decrease, making them comparable to their White counterparts of the same income levels.

Out of the twenty in-depth interviews with clients in Sheila's shop, ten women had experienced divorce. Divorce was not a desired outcome for any of these women or their children, but it was deemed the best alternative in light of their situations. Even though several studies have noted the negative effects of divorce, particularly for the children, there also is research that suggests that children are better off having their parents divorce than remaining in homes where there are high levels of marital conflict or violence.[8]

A married woman with three children described the status of families as such:

> I don't know if I want to just characterize it as just the Black family or just families. I think the same thing that is going on with Black families is going on with White families. It [family life] is being destroyed! My life is centered around the Lord, so I'm going to talk about God. When you leave God out of your situation, your life, and family, then it's going to be down[hill] for the family. . . . I work in the school system, so I see Black children and White children; all of them are affected by what goes on at home.

This client pointed out that issues related to the family were not limited to Blacks in general. Most family experts would agree with this view, and some have gone as far as using several social indicators to evaluate what they believe to be the decline of the family. Such indicators have been said to include increasing divorce rates, lower fertility rates, the increase in outside employment for women, the decline of the nuclear family, the rise in age for first-time marriages, the decrease in family size, and the rise in cohabitation. For more traditional family sociologists, these indicators are seen as both a national and an international concern. Arguments regarding the status of families in general and whether they are declining or just changing are discussed in the following section using material by prominent family sociologists.

Sociologists' Stance

In his review "American Family Decline, 1960–1990," David Popenoe discusses the decline of the American family. Decline, according to Popenoe, is a weakening of the family as an institution, inhibiting it from carrying out its main functions of rearing children and providing affection and companionship to its members. His definition of the family includes single-parent households, nonmarrieds, and any family types with dependent children, which would also include same-sex couples with children. According to Popenoe, families have lost their functions, social power, and authority over their members.[9]

He evaluates the decline of the family in terms of demographic, institutional, and cultural changes. First, when looking at demographics, he argues that families have grown smaller in size, less stable, and shorter in life span. Second, Popenoe notes the decline in the institutional dimension of families. He is concerned by the drop in fertility, which averaged 3.7 children per woman in the late 1950s and had dropped to 1.9 per woman by 1990. According to Popenoe, this low fertility rate fell under the requirements for necessary population replacement. He also examines the decline in nuclear families, stating that in 1960, 42 percent of all families had a sole male breadwinner; by 1988, that figure had dropped to 15 percent; and today it is less than 11 percent.

In 1960, 19 percent of married women with children under the age of six worked outside the home, but by 1990, that figure had grown to 59 percent. According to Popenoe, this has led to a breakdown in economic interdependence and therefore weakened cohesion in marriages and families. In 1960, 88 percent of children lived with two parents, and by 1989, that number had dropped to 73 percent. The fastest-growing family form in recent years has been the single-parent family, with roughly 90 percent of these families being headed by women. In 1960, 5 percent of all births occurred to unmarried females, but by 1990, this number had climbed to 24 percent and by 2000 to approximately 27 percent.

With the median age of first marriages being approximately four years older for women in the 1990s compared to those of the 1960s, Popenoe suggests that today more women are being fulfilled as singles. He also points out that more people are cohabiting, noting the greater likelihood of cohabitating couples to separate.

Finally, Popenoe turns to the cultural aspect of family. He believes a strong sense of family identification, loyalty, and focus on the family are lacking in our society. Popenoe idealizes the 1950s as a nostalgic era in which both marriage rates and birthrates were high, divorce rates were low, and there was a sense of solidarity. His biggest concern seems to be for children, whom he sees as being affected the most by recent family trends.

Whether one agrees or disagrees with Popenoe's points, his perspective is important for two reasons. First, it allows us to compare Black women's views and perceptions of the status of the family, a smaller segment of the population, to national trends, research, and mainstream views—such as Popenoe's. Second, it raises the question of how much of an effect changes in the larger society have on the Black family in particular.

In agreement with Popenoe's description of American families, one divorced mother discussed her concerns with what she described as the decline of extended family support in helping to ensure strong Black families:

> They [families] are so fragmented, even with the system of grandparents raising the children. Now grandparents are doing their own thing. Now everybody is sitting back. We need to get back to where we used to know that a grandparent or another family member would step in and help raise the children.

This woman pointed out what she saw as a recent decline of extended family support. She and several of the women pointed out the need for more extended family support, especially from grandparents. It is interesting to note that many Black families expect grandparents to help raise children, whereas in many other racial and ethnic families, this assistance is seen as more of a bonus than a necessity.

A client with four adult children vocalized her dissatisfaction with modern families.

> It's really very dysfunctional! Black families are nothing like they use to be. Parents used to be in the home more, and relatives and friends and family kinds of things were major events. I think now its more the kids raising or doing things that the parents should do. . . . When I grew up, kids did not talk back to their parents. The parents were there and they were the discipline and you knew exactly what you should and should not do. . . . [Today] kids are more or less raising their parents.

This mother of four was raised in the fifties and, like Popenoe, believed that family relations were much better back then. She believed that modern parents are not doing their jobs, and as a result families are becoming more and more dysfunctional.

Stephanie Coontz describes the 1950s as less than nostalgic. She argues that a combination of fifties sitcom reruns and an atypical decade of favorable marriage and family trends cemented an image in the brains of many

Americans of the 1950s as "the good old days." Coontz points out that while there was an increase in marriages, a decline in divorces, and a rise in fertility, the fifties family was a fluke based on a unique and temporary combination of economic, social, and political factors. Although many of the media images of this time showed middle-class wealth and traditional nuclear families, she notes out that during this same time, at least a quarter of the population was living in poverty, and those who were not in poverty often had to maintain dual incomes. This was especially the case for minority women.[10]

According to Coontz, many women were bullied into roles of wife and mother, because strong social stigmas were given to women who did not. Men were also pressured into being responsible and marrying early. Betty Friedan's 1963 book the *Feminine Mystique* was a testament of women experiencing identity conflicts after deciding that domestic duties were not all they wanted in life.

Judith Stacey states that children are suffering serious deprivations in the United States. She notes that women trying to raise children in single-parent homes are at a disadvantage financially. However, she cautions against using benchmark stereotypes of the past as a baseline for measuring further declines. Stacey suggests that our view of family must be inclusive of our changing society. She argues that conservative views, which suggest that women have to go back into the home for the family to survive, offer a myopic view of the real problem.[11]

A minister's wife and mother of five described Black families, in contrast to Coontz's and Stacey's views, in this way:

> Struggling! The majority are struggling. It's almost like a cycle. I don't agree with Louis Farrakahn, but I agree with the Million Man March, because the Black man has lost his role. My dad, growing up, worked hard for what we had. We didn't have much, but he worked hard. A lot of these men lack initiative. They have given up. Now these women have to be the head of the household, but that's not the way it is supposed to be. That's why I think the Black family is having so much problems. It's not going to get better until the Black man takes back his role as the head of the household.

Several of the clients felt that the answer to stronger Black families was in having Black men present in the home and, for Christian women in particular, having them demonstrating more spiritual leadership in the home. The women believed that the presence of Black men was needed to provide positive Black role models for African American boys, as well as to take some of the employment and financial burden off of Black women.

Philip Cowan suggests that with a rapidly changing economy, dual-career families are more and more of a necessity. In response to this change, Cowan proposes the need for more family policies that would enable parents to spend time with their children without the fear of being fired. He also cites research that indicates that both working mothers and their children could benefit from the mom working outside the home.[12]

For most working-class African American mothers, whether to stay home with their children has never been an option. Precarious employment and economic conditions have often left Black women with one option: work— or else have themselves and their children starve. Even when a husband is present, a Black woman often has to work to help maintain a livelihood for her family in a society that sometimes does and sometimes does not employ Black males.

While Sheila's clients supported two-parent households, whether dual-career or single-income, they expressed that two-parent households were not always possible. Several of the clients in the shop had experienced divorce or were unmarried. And although two-parent households were an ideal structure in which to raise children, these women had learned to make things work when ideals were not a reality. In such cases, they relied on extended family ties to help raise the children and support the mothers. One younger client stated, "People stress independence so much today that they forget they need interdependence. We need our families."

In a study done by Linda Blum and Theresa Deussen, Black working-class women utilized their extended family ties, which enabled them to feel more independent.[13] Feeling like they could not raise their children on their own, they often used extended family support to help raise their children. This was especially the case when the father of the child was not around to help raise the child. Although the women in Blum and Deussen's study did not express a desire to marry or rely on a man as a breadwinner, the women in Sheila's shop clearly stressed the need and importance of two-parent African American families.

Structural changes occurring in families today do not negate the fact that there are some problems families have to address, whether Black or White. As noted by various marriage and family scholars, there has been a steady rise in the divorce rate and in the number of single-parent households over the past several decades. These two trends have been particularly significant, because of the financial implications they have for women and children. Divorced women who are heads of households and children coming from single heads of households have a greater likelihood of living in poverty or near poverty.[14]

According to some, the trends mentioned here mean the family is declining, while for others it is merely changing. Whether one sees these changes or declines as good or bad is probably largely contingent on one's values, but whether one supports a one-parent or two-parent family, one thing is certain: Black families, both two-parent and single, have survived a deluge of obstacles and challenges and will continue to do so. Beverly Greene, a psychologist, says it best in an essay on African Americans' vulnerability and resilience:

> African American families have functioned under a legacy of challenges to their survival, beginning with slavery when families were not allowed to exist and when they were continually disrupted by abrupt and permanent separations. Surviving these disruptions, African American families have continued to demonstrate their flexibility and resilience under many adverse circumstances. African Americans are . . . survivors of historical and contemporary circumstances that may increase their vulnerability. However, as survivors they have much to teach us about resilience.[15]

Black Communities

In addition to the state of their families, clients in Sheila's shop talked about the strengths and weaknesses within Black communities and some of the biggest threats that affected Black families in these communities. The women focused on both positive and negative circumstances within their families and communities and what needed to occur to improve them.

Strengths

Sheila's clients pointed out several strengths within Black communities. Some of these strengths were emphasized more than once by several of the women. One such recurring strength was Black people's faith in God. One client stated, "Blacks have historically been religious people, and that is what kept us together. I think being religious people got us through slavery and difficult times." The women generally believed that their faith in God had brought them through harsh times.

Another client stated:

> I think that the church [is a strength]. We are very religious-oriented people. Even if we are not active churchgoers, we do believe in God, and we still have a Bible at home. So I think that one of our saving graces is that our children go to church. In that respect we are very family-oriented people. We are [also] very loyal people.

This client felt that African Americans' active involvement in church and religious affiliations was the source of strong family ties. From a different angle, one teacher simply stated, "We are survivors!" She continued by saying:

> I think our strength is that a lot of us have a sense of humor. We have learned to laugh off the hurt, and the people that have not learned to laugh off the hurt have learned to drink off the hurt. The drinking and the alcohol is because people are wounded, and they don't know how to survive the hurt. I [also] think our strength is our work ethic. Most [Black] people feel good about working.

Although African Americans have different ways of coping with the pain that has been inflicted on them by society, this woman felt that African Americans were still strong survivors and commended them for it. She believed that Blacks had overcome many obstacles and were still able to carry on. The women all identified habits of surviving as strengths that helped them to press through difficult times.

A client who is a social worker stated, "Blacks can ban together, when there's a problem. They do come together, and that's a strength!" Several of the women stated that Black people knew how to come together when they really needed to. Although many of the women felt that Blacks have not really come together since the civil rights movement, they still maintained that Blacks could unify and work together toward a common goal. An example that the women gave was the Million Man March of 1995, in which hundreds of thousands of Black men marched in Washington, D.C., to unify and show their zeal to improve their lives, families, and communities.

Weaknesses

The women pointed out several areas that needed improvement in the Black community. Areas that were considered weak included the lack of fathers present in homes, environmental deterioration in Black communities, competition and jealousy among Blacks, economic and employment situations, and the school system in Black communities. One client who is a school nurse stated:

> I see a challenge to see what we can do to help our Black children want to be educated. [They think] school is a social place to go socialize with their friends, and when they get there, they do nothing. It's sad. It hurts to see that. My oldest son, when he was in high school, he was in honors classes, and just about the only one. The only Black student and definitely around the only Black young man. When he graduated, he was the only Black student that graduated

with high honors. We have just as much intelligence as everybody else; it's just not being focused. We are not seeing that it's what we need. The school system does not work with them. I see a lot that was taken away from the Black community when segregation came about. I don't see us any further ahead than when we were back then.

This client felt that Blacks had failed to make the most of their education and that the school system had failed to meet the educational needs of Blacks.

In addition to educational woes, it was interesting to find that several of the women felt that racial integration had left some negative outcomes within Black communities. They were not proposing segregation, but they did see certain strengths and assets that had been taken out of Black communities when racial integration took place. One of these assets that was perceived as being lost was a sense of ownership in Black communities. These women believed that integration had fragmented the solidarity of their communities and left them with no place to really call their own. Another perceived loss was the weak education that African American children received. Inner-city schools in which the educators were White were deemed to be less than committed to inner-city African American children.

Another weakness that received heavy emphasis from the women was the state of African American men. One older divorced woman stated, "The Black men are on drugs, in prison; half of them have been killed due to drugs, or they have umpteen women. . . . Why would I want someone I have to share? Like I said, where else can you go but to the Lord?"

As the women talked, it became apparent that they were not out to bash Black men, but rather they were saddened by what had happened to many African American men and what patterns seemed to be being repeated by younger Black men. Many of these Black women felt that they had to carry much of the responsibility for their families but would have preferred a man to help to carry this responsibility. However, since this was not a reality in the lives of some of these women, they had readjusted their lives in the warrior mode and expected little change in their circumstances in the near future.

Finally, another problem identified by other Blacks about the Black community is the fact that Blacks spend a lot of disposable income on image-enhancing products, such as designer labels and shoes. While these items may make some feel good about themselves and stimulate the economy through consumption, they do very little for helping Blacks build, sustain, and return wealth to their own communities.

In *The Black Underclass*, Douglas Glasgow stipulates the importance of Black professionals such as administrators, engineers, and technologists to attend to the needs of their own communities, but he acknowledges that they are usually too busy meeting the demands of their own professional roles and mainstream life. As a result, he states, their knowledge has had little impact on treating the ills of the Black community. Instead, their expertise goes to the benefit of mainstream society.[16] Many Blacks regard this situation as a definite problem.

Biggest Threat

When asked what the biggest threat was in the Black community, several of the women talked about the symptoms of the drug problem, but when looking at the root of the drug problem, issues of joblessness, low incomes, and poor communities surfaced. A young police officer stated:

> We need to go back to the church. As far as our weaknesses, it's drugs and violence. We're killing ourselves. They don't have to wait on the White man to kill us, we're killing each other. And that's why there are so many ABCs [a liquor store] and [other] liquor stores in the Black community, because when they get to drinking they forget everything and nothing matters.

The identification of self-destructive forces in African American communities, such as an abundance of liquor stores in their neighborhoods, was pointed out by the clients. They saw it as a way in which society helped Blacks to destroy themselves.

When asked what the greatest need was in the Black community, a worker in her fifties said, "The need for better housing [for Blacks] and increase their income, that would help. Jobs are needed in the area, because some of them don't have cars." Economic concerns were seen as one of the biggest inhibitors to families functioning well. Still another young woman felt that by far the biggest threat within Black communities was "not seeing our own uniqueness, and so our self-worth is gone." This client felt that the biggest threat to Black communities was in Blacks accepting the labels that society had given them and becoming apathetic toward their present situations and future.

These weaknesses, according to the cumulative lived experiences concept, are the result of years of hegemonic practices toward Blacks, causing Blacks to act out in less than healthy ways. The women made the connection between stronger families and better communities in relation to combating tensions among Black people themselves, which calls for improved relationships. These relationships are discussed in the following section.

Relationships

Aside from families and communities, the women talked specifically about how Black women related to each other and how they related to Black men. Many of the women vocalized their concerns about Black males, as well as pointed out the positive attributes and important role of Black men. Some of these views are captured here.

Black Men

In one of her vocal moments, Sassy had this to say about Black men: "Contrary to what everybody believes, not all Black men are puppies [dogs]. Some Black men are true men. They love their families, and they are doing the right thing. They are good role models for their sons and their daughters." Like Sassy, many of the women felt that Black men had received a bad reputation. Sassy wanted to set the record straight by acknowledging the many good Black men who existed.

Joan Morgan states that believing the myth that all men are dogs reinforces and condones irresponsible behavior, because it puts the blame on gender instead of individual choice and upbringing.[17] Each individual is responsible for making his or her own choices whether male or female, and within those groupings some make primarily good choices and some bad. Morgan puts some of the blame on women, encouraging them to raise their sons and not just love them. It is more difficult to have an irresponsible man if he wasn't allowed to be an irresponsible boy.

Morgan also points out that just as there was the myth of the Strongblackwoman, there was also the myth of "Endangeredblackman." She states that Black women coddle Black men, believing the lie that they are weaker than Black women and less capable of standing on their own or enduring hardships.[18] This phenomenon seems to cause some Black women to "settle" for men that they have little in common with or respect for. Morgan suggests instead that in their relationships with Black men, Black women need to focus on their "standards" and forget about the notion of settling.

One client who seemed to inadvertently endorse the Endangeredblackman ideology stressed the fact that Black women needed to trust Black men more.

> Black women have a tendency not to trust their Black men, and as a result they don't build them up—they tear them down. . . . If we started treating our little boys as we would want them to be as our husbands, start training them early, then it would make a big difference. This will be somebody's husband someday.

Help him to know how to treat his sister, and then he will know how to treat his girlfriend [or wife] one day.

Many of Sheila's clients talked about the challenges that they believed Black men faced in society and the need for Black women to support them more and to raise younger African American males to be productive and responsible when they became adults.

Lisa Jones states the media have Black women fighting over what statistics identify as a dwindling supply of Black men. She says this is so much so that some Black women are willing to settle for someone else's leftovers, or what she in jest describes as the "one-in-four problem": one out of every four Black men is in jail, number two is on drugs, number three prefers men or blondes, and number four already has ten women.[19]

In her article "Taking Sides against Ourselves," Rosemary Bray discusses the mixed loyalties that Black women often face in their relationships.[20] She suggests that Black men and White women frequently make claims to the loyalties of Black women but that Black women are often in a no-win situation, pitting gender issues against race. Bray goes on to state that when a side has to be chosen, Black women are more likely to choose to be loyal to their race rather than their gender. According to Bray, Anita Hill, an African American law professor who at one time worked with Supreme Court Justice Clarence Thomas and accused him of sexual harassment, breached the ultimate taboo when she openly downgraded a Black man in a courtroom filled with White men. This was an indictment serious enough to constitute the excommunication of Hill from her race. For many Black women, choosing to support Black males sometimes to the exclusion of their own needs is a difficult decision. The gendered racism concept addresses the double burden that Black women face, which puts them at odds with their Black brothers on gender issues and causes them to reject their gender when it comes to race issues.

Black Women

When looking at how Black women related to other Black women, something of a contradiction arose among the women I interviewed. Several of the women seemed to state a general distrust of Black women. Reasons given included competition over available Black men and Black women being jealous over the personal accomplishments of other Black women. The clients were somewhat mistrusting of other Black women to whom they were not related. Although they openly affirmed the supportive networks that they had with other women in the beauty shop, in their churches, and in their community organizations, they seemed to be suspicious of women they did not know. "Strange" women had to be watched carefully; after all, they could be men snatchers or other types of deviants. Somehow the Black women they knew personally were different from the women they only knew vaguely.

A single woman described Black female relationships like this:

> [Either they are] very close to each other and best friends, or they see each other as enemies. I think it should be a sisterhood among us. I'm not married, like I said, but if you're dating, I don't need to be trying to get your man. We always feel like we have to have a rivalry between us.

This competition over "a few good men" seemed to be at the center of much of the rivalry among Black women. Although men often felt pressured to do well in society professionally, women often felt pressured to do well relationally. This motivated some women to get into relationships at any cost, even if it meant destroying another woman's relationship in the process.

One woman saw Black female relationships as being fine until one started to succeed. "I think there is a lot of camaraderie, if they [Black women] are in the same situation. We know that all of us are struggling. I also have seen them perceive you as a threat. They see you succeeding and view you as a threat, which is not helpful." This woman pointed out the role of equality in maintaining good Black female relationships. As long as two Black women saw themselves as equals, they were able to get along well, but the moment one was perceived as doing better, the relationship often crumbled. Although several women thought Black female relationships were fine, they also saw room for improvement. These women saw the need for Black women to see each other as assets and resources rather than as part of the competition, to learn to support each other in successes and not just sufferings.

K. Sue Jewell stresses the importance to African American women of creating and being a part of social networks that allow them to support each other and to strengthen the cause and image of Black women as a whole. Unity does not necessarily mean uniformity.[21] Black women can maintain their individual uniqueness, but instead of promoting rivalry and competition, they can empower each other by refusing to let any Black woman be disrespected in the media or otherwise, by raising sons to treat Black women with respect, and by passing on to their daughters the fact that Black females are one of their greatest allies.

The Gender Divide

When asked to discuss their perception of who had it hardest, Black men or Black women, fourteen of the twenty Black women stated that Black men had it hardest. One client stated:

> I think Black men have it a lot harder. Society is intimidated by the Black male, and as a result they are treated differently. It's a lot harder for them. They [society] don't feel as intimidated by women for some reason, so things are a lot easier for women.

Out of the five women who stated that Black women had things harder, one woman said:

> I would say the Black woman, because Black women have to be strong for Black men and also for their children. We're the only support that the Black man has. Black men don't have the same opportunities as White men, if they did, a lot of Black women wouldn't have to work like they do. The Black man doesn't get paid as much as White men do. So we definitely have to be strong for our husbands and our children.

Only one woman believed that both Black men and Black women had it equally hard. "I think both Black men and Black women have difficult times, but in different ways. I think the struggle is equally divided." Regardless of who had it hardest, in the end the women concluded that Black men and women really did need each other and had to raise the cause of each other in order to raise the cause and conditions of African American families and communities.

Theoretical Conclusions

The three theoretical concepts are discussed here in light of specific topics that were addressed within this chapter. First, the cumulative lived experiences concept is useful in helping us better understand the *weaknesses* and the *biggest threats* within Black communities that were discussed in this chapter. Based on this view, problems with drugs, crime, and Black father absenteeism are merely the results of the historically poor social and economic treatment of Blacks. Community social problems are therefore indicators of institutionally racist structures that have inhibited Black men, Black families, and ultimately Black communities from being empowered and self-sufficient.

Second, the gendered racism concept exposes the dilemma of many Black women. Often made to feel at odds with Black men by society and accused of taking jobs away from Black men, Black women face gender alienation within their families and communities. This gender alienation, or separation of positive interactions between Black women and Black men, often leaves Black women feeling like they are in a no-win situation. If they succeed, they are said to be stealing success from the Black man, but if they fail, they are made to be scapegoats for the social and economic ills of the broader society.

Finally, the habit of surviving concept aids us in seeing the strength of Black families. Whether both parents are present or not, these Black women's strong commitment to familialism is seen as they raise their own children and sometimes those of others with the help of extended family and fictive kin. These women have chosen to be survivors and thrivers in terms of their gender, class, and race. In the following chapter, the women discuss the concept of race in fuller detail.

Notes

1. U.S. Census Bureau, *Census 2000 Summary File 4 (SF4) Sample Data* (Washington, D.C.: U.S. Government Printing Office, 2000).

2. William J. Wilson, *When Work Disappears: The World of the New Urban Poor* (New York: Knopf, 1996).

3. Jesse McKinnon, *The Black Population in the United States: March 2002*, Current Population Reports, Series P20–541 (Washington, D.C.: U.S. Census Bureau, 2003); Arlene Saluter, "Marital Status and Living Arrangements: March, 1993," in *Bureau of the Census Current Population Reports* (Washington, D.C.: U.S. Government Printing Office, 1994), 20.

4. M. B. Tucker and R. J. Taylor, "Demographic Correlates of Relationship Status among Black Americans," *Journal of Marriage and the Family* 51 (1989): 655–65; Robert Staples, ed., *The Black Family: Essays and Studies*, 3d ed. (Belmont, Calif.: Wadsworth, 1988); William J. Wilson, *The Truly Disadvantaged* (Chicago: University of Chicago Press, 1987); Wilson, *When Work Disappears*.

5. The women only discussed marriage and family within the context of heterosexuality.

6. David Newman, *Sociology of Families* (Thousand Oaks, Calif.: Pine Forge, 1999); Saluter, "Marital Status and Living Arrangements: March, 1993."

7. Helen Raschke, "Divorce," in *Handbook of Marriage and the Family*, ed. Marvin Sussman and Suzanne Steinmetz (New York: Plenum, 1987); Frank Cox, *Human Intimacy*, 7th ed. (St. Paul, Minn.: West, 1996).

8. Paul Allison and Frank Furstenberg, "How Marital Dissolution Affects Children: Variations by Age and Sex," *Developmental Psychology* 25 (1989): 540–49.

9. David Popenoe, "American Family Decline, 1960–1990: A Review and Appraisal," *Journal of Marriage and the Family* 55 (1993): 527–41.

10. Stephanie Coontz, *The Way We Never Were* (New York: Basic Books, 1992).

11. Judith Stacey, "Good Riddance to the Family: A Response to Popenoe," *Journal of Marriage and the Family* 55 (1993): 545–47.

12. Philip Cowan, "The Sky is Falling, but Popenoe's Analysis Won't Help Us Do Anything about it," Journal of Marriage and the Family 55 (1993): 548–52. Also see Philip Cowan and Carolyn Cowan, *When Partners Become Parents* (New York: Basic Books, 1992).

13. Linda Blum and Theresa Dreussen, "Negotiating Independent Motherhood: Working-class African American Women Talk about Marriage and Motherhood," *Gender & Society* 10 (1996): 199–211.

14. Felix Berardo, "Family Research in the 1980s: Recent Trends and Future Directions," in *Contemporary Families*, ed. Alan Booth (Minneapolis: National Council on Family Relations, 1990); Popenoe, "American Family Decline."

15. Beverly Greene, "African American Families: A Legacy of Vulnerability and Resilience," in *Annual Editions Marriage and Family 1999/2000* (Guilford, Conn.: Dushkin/McGraw-Hill, 1999), 29.

16. Douglas Glasgow, *The Black Underclass: Poverty, Unemployment, and Entrapment in Ghetto Youth* (San Francisco: Jossey-Bass, 1980).

17. Joan Morgan, *When Chickenheads Come Home to Roost: My Life as a Hip Hop Feminist* (New York: Simon & Schuster, 1999).

18. Morgan, *When Chickenheads Come Home to Roost.*

19. Lisa Jones, *Bulletproof Diva: Tales of Race, Sex, and Hair* (New York: Doubleday, 1994).

20. Rosemary Bray, "Taking Sides against Ourselves," *New York Times Magazine* 141 (November 17, 1991), 56ff.

21. K. Sue Jewell, *From Mammy to Miss America and Beyond: Cultural Images and the Shaping of U.S. Social Policy* (New York: Routledge, 1993), 13.

CHAPTER FOUR

Racial Matters

Experiencing everyday racism may come down to taking or putting up with incidents without protest. When faced with the argument that they are "hypersensitive," Blacks often feel that there is nothing they can say. Furthermore, Whites often do not recognize their own racism, or simply deny it outright. As a result, Blacks who broach the subject of covert racism may feel they are treading on thin ice.

—Philomena Essed, *Everyday Racism*

MS. FOSTER: I was reading about Abraham [in the Bible].
WOMEN: Uh-hmm.
MS. FOSTER: And his son, the son he had with him. . . .
SHEILA: Hagar.
MS. FOSTER: (excitedly) Yeah, Hagar!
SHEILA: Ishmael.
MS. FOSTER: [Yes,] Ishmael. . . . I think we are descendants of Ishmael.
SHEILA: You know what, a lot of people say that, and they say that's why we're cursed because they are like . . .
KIM: They said that about Ham, too.
SHEILA: Yeah. Talkin' about Ham got cursed and it came down to us. Because Noah was drunk and Ham saw his nakedness and he told them he would be cursed all of his days and so [they say Blacks are cursed] . . . and I say no because when Jesus' blood was applied to my life, that curse was broken!
KIM: . . . You know my godmother used to say that. She said, Black people are cursed because they are descendants of Ham and they were dark people.

And I said, "Well they were dark before they got cursed so the curse doesn't have anything to do with their blackness!" That means Adam and Eve must have been dark. People just had color!

MS. FOSTER: (sarcastically) The only curse in the Bible that had to do with color was when Mariam was cursed with leprosy. And that wasn't dark—that was light!

WOMEN: (excitedly) That's right!

MS. FOSTER: And one of Abraham's wives was Black.

KIM: (enthusiastically) And David, too, David had some Black concubines.

SHEILA: (joining in) And Moses' wife was Black.

WOMEN: (unanimous support) Yeah!

This chapter looks at the women's perceptions of racial matters in America. The women discuss government policies regarding African Americans, their experiences with discrimination, and how "everyday" racism has affected them.

A Matter of Color

The cumulative lived experiences concept points to an everyday skill that Blacks often utilize called the *second eye*. As explained in the introduction, the second eye refers to the process whereby people of color look at a situation from a dual perspective. It involves interpreting situations, comments, and human interactions not only from the perspective of an American but also as an African American. Although racist experiences from the past had caused some of Sheila's clients' second eye to be more sensitive to acts of racism, most of the women tried to give people and events the benefit of the doubt. Here, the clients discuss how racial relations have changed and in some cases stayed the same.

A secretary stated her concerns about racial relations: "I think there is a big problem with racial matters in America today. I think a lot of people are trying to look over the problem and not deal with it face on. I don't like it. I don't like what I see. . . . There's a big problem with racism in our society." This client, as well as some of the others, was upset by the fact that racial relations were often portrayed more positively than they actually were. She believed that while mainstream society believed that racial relations were better than ever, those who have lived in the margins of society, namely, minorities, saw things far differently.

When asked about current racial matters in America, one client stated, "It's sad that I can't tell much difference in racism from segregation to integration." She and several other clients were disappointed with the lack of racial progress, as well as with the disappointing reality that integration had not produced more progressive outcomes than what was present in society.

A Gallup poll released in June 1997 just after I completed my interviews with Sheila's clients found that a third of all Blacks surveyed believed that racial relations between Blacks and Whites had become worse by the late 1990s.[1] In another poll taken by the Joint Center for Political and Economic Studies, only 22 percent of African Americans felt that race relations were good in their communities, compared to 59 percent of White respondents.[2]

The difference in racial outlook can be partly explained by the fact that at any given time Black unemployment rates are much greater than those of Whites. Black men also experience higher rates of incarceration than White men, and the proportion of Black men in prison is approximately twenty times the corresponding rate for White men.[3] At any given moment, about 25 percent of African American men between the ages of twenty and twenty-nine are imprisoned, on probation, or on parole.[4] The playing fields for Blacks and Whites seem to be vastly different.

When looking specifically at African Americans and health, according to international health reports, the United States ranks below many western-ized nations in the overall quality of life, following such countries as Japan and several European countries. Poor African Americans have been identi-fied as receiving very few benefits from America's mainstream society and economy, and if considered separately from White America, poor African Americans and other poor Americans would rank more closely in overall quality of life with the poorest of the poor, such as those in sub-Saharan Africa. Based on these and other statistics, for many Blacks, when it comes to health and wealth, there are two separate Americas, one for Whites and one for Blacks.[5]

In his research on race and health, David R. Williams found that African Americans were more likely to die from many of the leading causes of death, including the two leading causes, heart disease and cancer, than any other racial or ethnic group in the United States. They were also the highest group represented in other categories of sickness and death such as diabetes, HIV/AIDS, and homicide. According to Williams, these higher death rates possibly indicate higher levels of ill health among African Americans, differences in access to health care, and possible disparities in medical treatment—all of which are affected by socioeconomic status; however, his research also points to the positive correlation between discrimination and poorer health among African Americans.[6]

With these and other factors in mind, the women in the shop felt that so-cietal race relations were not as good as they could be. Each of the women had experienced some negative racial encounters, and although the women felt like they did not go looking for racism, they pointed out that racial incidents found them. One woman stated, "I feel that most people don't want to admit that there is a problem, but there is. It's not that you go looking for them, but when it's presented to you, and it's right in your face, you can't help but notice that it is a Black and White issue."

The cumulative lived experiences concept points out that it is not sporadic incidents of racism that cause African Americans to be hostile toward society, but rather the accumulation of everyday racism that eventually causes Blacks to become intolerant of oppressive practices. As the client stated earlier, most Blacks do not go looking for racist situations, but they do not necessarily just walk away from them, either. Author Gloria Yamato compares the problem of racism to that of a virus, noting that by the time one comes up with a cure, it's mutated to a new resistant form.[7]

When asked about the effects of racism, one client discussed her fear associated with racism: "It's had its effect down through the years, even from a child, all the way up. In the beginning it puts a barrier there. A fear comes. But then you determine what you are going to be, and you walk over that barrier of fear and move forward . . . otherwise you will be left behind." Racism was sometimes intimidating to some of the women, but learning to deal with it head-on seemed to be the secret to these women overcoming its negative impact. While this did not stop racist attitudes, it did help the women overcome some of the negative effects that racism had on them. Although most of the women did not see racism as necessarily curable, they did believe that they could inoculate themselves and their children against some of its harmful effects by their positive outlook on life.

Margaret Andersen and Patricia Hill Collins state, "Racism is not the same thing as prejudice, although prejudice is one manifestation of racism. The concept of institutional racism reminds us that racism is not just a matter of belief but is also embedded in a system of power relations."[8] Fundamentally in agreement with this statement, many of Sheila's clients believed that racism was institutionally ingrained within the American culture and not something that could be readily removed.

According to Joe Feagin and Clairece Feagin, institutional racism is often subtle in its discriminatory practices. These authors state that while subtle discrimination practices were obvious to the victim, the internalization of racist ideas and acts by White employers had led many organizations to endorse discriminatory behavior unbeknownst to them at least at a conscious level.[9]

Berniece, one of Sheila's clients who is married to a pastor, recounted a racial encounter not in the workplace but in her community.

We live in this mostly White neighborhood. When we moved there, we decided to go to this White church. They made my husband the pastor of the church. So here we are in this small town that was very prejudiced, and my husband was pastoring mostly older White people. We discussed issues that a lot of them came out with. They said that they were prejudiced, but they were working on it. I'm glad that we had that experience. Even in the church people are trying, but they've been White all their lives! Right now those people love us to death, in an area where people are still writing KKK on your door.

Having had to face prejudice and racism in a variety of different settings, most of the women believed that good could come out of Blacks and Whites interacting with each other and learning from each other. When possible, many of the women utilized their power of influence to help foster positive relationships between Blacks and Whites.

Mary, an older client, identified what she saw as some racial progress.

I can say that they [racial relations] are better than they were ten years ago, but there's a lot of room for improvement. Things are better than when I was growing up. See, when I was growing up, we didn't have the opportunities that African Americans have today, but still there's room for improvement.

Although most of the clients would agree that Blacks in today's society have more opportunities than Blacks did in the 1950s and 1960s, they would also agree that race relations still need some improvement.

One such area in which the clients thought racial relations could be improved was in exposing and eliminating racist stereotypes. Many of them believed that African Americans were often viewed negatively when they were collectively interacting with each other. They pointed out that it was not uncommon for a large congregation of Blacks to draw suspicion of gang activity, rioting, or plans to rob or revolt against an establishment. One client stated:

It seems like when people of color are huddled together, like males huddled together, people think that they are going to start something, but they are just getting together to stand around and talk. There are a lot of misconceptions. When young Black males get together and young Black females get together, it's not always for bad stuff.

Large groups of Blacks congregating together often made non-Blacks feel as though some illegal or deviant activity was taking place. Many of these racist misconceptions are historically rooted in stereotypical images of African Americans as deviants and genetic or pathological misfits.[10] These stereotypical disbeliefs can be traced back to slavery, when slave masters worked diligently to polarize their slaves to minimize the possibility of mutiny.

In Living Color

One large arena in which many of these stereotypes have been acted out has been the media, as noted in chapter 2. But more specifically, when looking at television, the women discussed how they felt that Black men, in addition to Black women, were largely stereotyped on television. Stereotypes of Black men were often associated with crime and violence, while stereotypes of Black women were largely associated with servitude and lasciviousness. Some examples of negative stereotypes of Black women have included inaccurate statements in the media such as "The majority of welfare recipients are Black women," "Black women have several children by several different men," and "Black women are seducers and sexually promiscuous."

Daily news reports have insisted on discussing problems with welfare while showing a Black face. This has been in spite of the fact that, numerically, White women make up the majority of welfare recipients. Other sources of stereotypes are historical myths or folklore that have been passed down from one generation to the next. Although rarely acknowledged, Feagin and Vera note that these historically racist ideologies actually came at a high price to the mental well-being of those Whites who perpetuated them.[11]

Even though Blacks have been given bad publicity in the media, it must be noted that Black producers, actors, and promoters have also taken the artistic liberty to make fun of Blacks in what might be seen as an exploitive manner. Such television shows as In Living Color and Black music videos might be considered prime examples. In Spike Lee's movie Bamboozled (2000), he highlights the fact that Blacks sometimes reinforce stereotypical images of themselves in the name of profit or success. Although mostly done in jest or in joyful recognition of a nonmonocultural group of people, such actions nevertheless contribute to the problem. This being said, I must emphasize that Blacks making fun of Blacks, no matter how funny or distasteful, is a far cry from ongoing acts of institutional racism that have negative political, social, and economical implications for an entire race of people. If society is concerned about the future well-being of African American people and their communities, it must also be concerned about raising the status of African Americans in the media.[12] In the following section, I look at ways in which racial hostilities have been frequently acted out both in the lives of Sheila's clients and in the larger social milieu.

Disabling Discrimination

Discrimination supersedes prejudice and stereotyping in that it not only involves ungrounded and negative misconceptions, attitudes, and beliefs but also moves one step further into acting on these beliefs. Examples of discrimination have been numerous in this country, including everything from forced assimilation to the exclusion of certain groups from acquiring home loans. In short, while many Americans do not consider themselves to be prejudiced, they often act on prejudical ideas when a situation threatens their status quo or community.

The cumulative lived experiences concept proposes that continuous acts of discrimination eventually lead to a reaction. This view was evident among the women at the shop. On any given day Sheila's clients talked candidly about their experiences with discrimination and how they felt and responded to discriminatory situations. Several of the clients shared their encounters with discrimination in such places as the workplace, academic settings, car dealerships, restaurants, and stores. One woman said, "Whenever I go to the shopping malls, I am discriminated against. I can go into a store, and people will automatically come and walk up to me, and I know a lot of times it's because I'm a Black person." Most of the women described what they saw as harassment in department stores, which was often displayed through overwatchfulness by store salespeople or, at the other extreme, being ignored all together. Sheila's sister-in-law Burnadette described an incident that had both angered and humiliated her.

> The only thing that really aggravates me is being followed in the store. I went to the dollar store one day, just as it was about to close, and the girl working in the store said, "We're going to be closing in about ten minutes." So I said, "No problem, I only came to get one thing." So as I went down the aisle, someone began to follow me. I don't know if they felt like since I came into the store right before it closed that maybe I was coming to steal or something, but they followed me in the store. And they didn't have what I was looking for, so that made me mad, because I really wanted to buy what I was looking for so that they didn't think that I was coming in here to see what I could get. . . . Just because I'm Black doesn't mean I'm going to steal! Don't put everybody in the same boat.

Common occurrences such as that Burnadette described made these women angry at the stereotypical images that many stores had of them, which lead to discriminatory treatment and humiliation.

Discrimination on the job was also a common occurrence. Job discrimination was manifested in different ways. When asked if she had ever been discriminated against, this police officer stated:

> Yes, as a matter of fact, promotions and different things at the job, they don't like to admit it, but it is a color barrier. You can be there longer than an officer or have just as much training, and they'll give the promotion to the White

officer. I look at it basically as discrimination, because I am Black and a female, and he is a White male, so he gets the promotion and I don't. When I question this, I get, "That's just the way it is!"

When it came to job promotions, discrimination was sometimes blatant. When the women challenged discriminatory promotion practices they were sometimes ignored, not taken seriously, or made to feel like their job security was in jeopardy. This threat of job security at times made it easier not to confront.

A client who worked for a mental health facility talked about her supervisors' control over Black colleagues' behavior.

> I started working for a mental health facility that was dealing with mentally ill persons. Within six months I was promoted on that job to the bed clinic coordinator. The person that I worked with, my direct supervisor, was . . . Caucasian. . . . There were only three Blacks in the workplace in the particular department that I worked with, and I saw what I considered to be racism to the point that they directly got rid of one girl. I was told to keep my nose out of the situation. . . . This girl was discriminated against. She wasn't allowed to use the phone. She was the secretary. How can you have a secretary that's not allowed to use the phone? The phone for her area was directed to a White secretary, and the Black lady was not allowed to use the phone! They did everything they could to make her quit. Eventually she did, but she was trying to make them fire her, so that she could collect unemployment. But eventually she was forced to quit, because they treated her so bad. It was racism. When I talked to the personnel director, she wanted to know if I felt like the girl was being discriminated against as an individual or racially, and I told her both, because she [the Black secretary] wasn't allowed to talk to me. . . . Eventually I quit, just because of the way they handled people.

This client relayed her displeasure with how her supervisors limited Black employee interactions because if they talked to each other, they might empower each other. This was just one of the many acts of discrimination that many of the women had encountered. The separation of Blacks in the workforce, the regulation of Black hair styles, and the exclusion of African apparel were all ways in which discrimination took shape in places of employment for Black women. Many of these women were forced to conform and play by the rules of their employers or find new jobs.

Sometimes discrimination is evident in how Black women are treated in comparison to how other workers are treated at their places of employment. A correctional officer discussed the differences in treatment for Black female workers.

Being Black and American, you will experience discrimination to a certain extent. A lot of times on my job, the men will want to treat you equal, like you
are a man, while they treat White women much better. It's like we are tough
and can deal with whatever, whereas the White women are treated more frag-
ilely. That I see a lot. To a certain extent it hurts, because I'm still a woman
like their mother or any other lady.

As this woman and several scholars have pointed out, Black women and
White women are often treated differently in the workplace. Philomena
Essed found that Black women were often perceived more like male equiva-
lents on job sites than as women.[13] But being treated equal to a man was not
so much the problem as having one's femininity overlooked on account of
one's race. K. Sue Jewell points out that since Black women have been associated with traditionally male attributes such as independence, strength, and
assertiveness, they have been masculinized in society and in the "Consciousness Industries" (mass media).[14]

Although the women in the shop did not recall specific incidents of discrimination as it related to housing, housing discrimination has also been a
problem for many Blacks. According to the Home Mortgage Disclosure Act
(HMDA), in the mid-1990s Blacks were denied Federal Housing Administration (FHA), Veterans Administration (VA), and conventional home
mortgages about twice as often as Whites. This rate was the same for home
improvement and refinancing loans. Even Blacks with high incomes were
turned down twice as often as Whites. Critics said this was because more people were applying for loans, some of whom were not eligible for loans.[15]

Feagin and Feagin identify four types of discrimination: isolated discrimination, small-group discrimination, direct institutionalized discrimination, and indirect discrimination, all of which have been experienced by
Sheila and her clients in one form or another. Feagin and Feagin define
these various types of discrimination in the following ways. First, *isolated
discrimination* is "harmful action taken intentionally by a member of a dominant racial group against members of a subordinate group, without the
support of other members of the dominant group in the immediate social
or community context."[16] One example of this type given by the women is
an individual waitress or waiter in a major restaurant choosing to ignore
them or their families, making them wait so long they finally leave the
restaurant.

Small-group discrimination is where "harmful action [is] taken intentionally
by a small number of dominant-group individuals acting in concert against
members of subordinate racial and ethnic groups, without the support of the
norms and of most other dominant group members in the immediate social

or community context."[17] An example of this type would be the same as the first example but on a larger scale. This is where you have collaborative efforts of several restaurant employees choosing to discriminate against certain customers without the approval or awareness of the restaurant owner.

Direct institutionalized discrimination is "an organizationally prescribed or community-prescribed action that by intention has a differential and negative impact on members of subordinate racial and ethnic groups." Feagin and Feagin suggest that these actions are usually routinely practiced by large numbers of the dominant group and are facilitated by legal or informal norms of the immediate organizational or community context.[18] An example of this form is Shoney's and Denny's restaurants' alleged discriminatory hiring, promotional, and customer treatment practices of minorities from top management down during the mid-1990s.

Finally, *indirect institutionalized discrimination* "consists of dominant-group practices having a harmful impact on members of subordinate racial and ethnic groups even though the organizationally or community-prescribed norms or regulations guiding those actions have been established with no intent to harm."[19] An example of this type would be where this same company has stated that it is committed to hiring "qualified" people of color, with educational credentials and experience equal to that of Whites. Its excuse for not having more Black workers is that Blacks just do not have the necessary qualifications.

In *Everyday Racism*, Essed narrows it down to two types of discrimination, direct and indirect.[20] She suggests that *direct discrimination* had to do with the familiar idea of unequal treatment in equal circumstances. For example, two women are applying for the same job, and both are equally qualified, but one is White and one is Black. But the White woman receives the job automatically because she is White, and the Black woman does not simply because she is Black. Although this is a hypothetical example, many merits and promotions have been traced to who one knew, as well as to one's physical appearance and traits such as race.

Indirect discrimination refers to "adverse effects on people of specific racial and ethnic descent, except that in this case the discrimination is due to equal treatment."[21] Essed believes this is a matter of equal enforcement of unequal procedures or rules. An example in the United States is standardized tests. Standardized tests are often used to measure one's scholastic ability or knowledge base, but the standard that is being used to judge the performance has largely been White and middle class.[22]

In *Understanding Everyday Racism*, Essed makes a further distinction about discrimination. She defines macro and micro dimensions of discrimination.

Macro discrimination is institutional, focusing on a system of structural inequities and historical practices. *Micro discrimination* focuses on individuals who utilize existing structural inequities in the system, thereby making them accomplices of a racist system.[23]

Although the women in Sheila's shop did not use these discrimination terms to describe their experiences with racism and unequal treatment, the fact was, according to them, racism and discrimination were realities that they had to deal with both personally and institutionally. Even though the women did not seek to make a racial incident out of every event, they did acknowledge the need for stores, restaurants, and employers to confront their own individual and institutional biases toward people of color to help ameliorate racial relations as a whole. In the following section, I look at one institutional way of dealing with racism and discrimination known as affirmative action.

Affirmative Action

HANK: (one of Sheila's few male clients who came in for a Jheri curl) I do have a problem with them overturning affirmative action, 'cause there's a lot of Black leaders in Congress and wherever else that have benefited from affirmative action, and now they're up . . .

KIM: Uh-huh.

HANK: . . . they look down on poor people and say, "Hey, we need to get rid of that [program]; we don't need to help these poor folks."

KIM: Yeah.

HANK: I got a problem with that.

KIM: OK. So you're saying a lot of Blacks have benefited from affirmative action, and now that they are high and lifted up, they want to just ban a lot of these programs?

HANK: Well, look at Keyes . . . what's his name? He got a talk show. The bald-headed guy from Chicago? These guys are Republican and they . . . oh, gee.

BURNADETTE: What, are you talking about that man . . . .

HANK: If you call his name, I can . . . .

KIM: Robert?

BURNADETTE: Robert?

HANK: No, they're both Black. Keyes was an ambassador during the Reagan administration, and he was a presidential candidate a couple of years ago—do you know who I'm talking about? . . . Uh, and this other guy from Chicago, bald-headed guy, Williams something. I mean these guys just totally forgot where they came from.

KIM: Hmm.

HANK: They came out of the projects, got an education, and now they are
like, "You shouldn't have no welfare and this and that and the other."
KIM: Yeah.
HANK: You got to help somebody. I do it all the time even though I'm getting critical. . . . But you got to reach back and pull up or at least try anyway.

During a time when affirmative action had been severely challenged and
programs intended to ameliorate racial conditions revoked, I asked the
women what they thought of this policy/program and whether they thought
affirmative action was still needed today. Some people have identified programs such as affirmative action as reverse discrimination, but according to
many proponents of affirmative action, reverse discrimination cannot occur
without key factors—namely, power and control. In addition, the cumulative
experiences concept suggests that long-term discrimination can be corrected
only through aggressive programs to counteract such harmful inequalities.
These points and others are addressed by the women themselves.

When looking at a government policy to eradicate racial discrimination,
the women were split in terms of the pros and cons of affirmative action.
While all of them felt that it was still needed, some of them felt that some
revisions were necessary. One client stated:

> One issue that is coming out a lot more is reverse discrimination. In some in-
> stances, I feel like reverse discrimination does happen, but to go and do away
> with affirmative action altogether. . . . I feel like there should be some kind of
> alternative to affirmative action. I feel like affirmative action should be up-
> dated to fit these times, but to do away with it all together would be inappro-
> priate. It would take us right back to the sixties, fifties, or forties, when things
> weren't fairly distributed. . . . People would not just naturally hire Blacks. . . .
> If affirmative action is abolished, then they will do it [not hire Blacks] openly
> and have no regards for our rights.

This woman felt like affirmative action was still needed. She was skeptical
about employers naturally hiring minorities without government interven-
tion. One client felt strongly about what she identified as quotas. "Businesses
shouldn't be required to hire a certain number of Blacks, because everyone
needs a job, and maybe more Blacks will need jobs than what the set number allows." Even though this woman believed that there needed to be government policy to assist Blacks in getting jobs, she was strongly against any
programs that mandated companies to hire a certain number or percentage
of minorities. Ultimately, she felt that Blacks would suffer in the end, with
companies hiring only the minimum amount.

The fear of digressing from the racial strides that the United States has already made seemed to loom in the minds of several women. One client stated:

> I feel like race matters are going back to like before the sixties. Racism seems to be creeping back up in a lot of different ways. Things that people fought for in the past, society seems to be more willing to let go . . . we're relinquishing the rights that so many people fought and died for. . . . I feel like reverse discrimination does happen, but to go and do away with it [affirmative action]? . . . People would not just naturally hire Blacks.

Even though the women believed that racial relations should have been stable enough to be able to do without affirmative action programs, they did not have much confidence in minority hiring practices without it. The question remained: Had less than forty years of policy programs been enough time to correct hundreds of years of wrongs?[24]

One client found it difficult to take a side on affirmative action. She felt that affirmative action had taken away Blacks' credibility for gaining a job due to qualifications and hard work. She stated:

> There has been a lot of controversy about the affirmative action program. A lot of people have said that they have gotten jobs because of the affirmative action and not because of merit alone. I really can't in all honesty address that because where I am at right now, I have really struggled and strived very hard to get there, and it is not an affirmative action type of thing. It's based on my merit of work alone.

Another client also discussed the assumption behind affirmative action.

> Well, I've been reading a little here and there about affirmative action and how they really want to rescind it and take it back. I don't think that they should. A lot of people think that Blacks get where they are because of the affirmative action and not because of their own merit. That person, if they have that position, they have earned that position. I know from my own experience of working in the workplace, a lot of times a Black person would put out ten times as much, and only every now and then will he or she get recognized. I think that it is very unfair for them to feel that if you finally get the position, it is only because of the affirmative action, when Black people are actually very productive in the workplace.

This woman strongly believed that with or without the help of affirmative action Blacks received positions due to their own merits and hard work. Although the women generally saw a need for affirmative action, the dilemma of having their abilities questioned as a result of it was difficult for them to live with.

The 1964 Civil Rights Act, under which affirmative action programs were born, prohibits discrimination because of race, color, sex, or national origin. It has been defined as "any effort taken to expand opportunity for women or racial, ethnic and national origin minorities by using membership in those groups that have been subject to discrimination as a consideration," and programs that fell under its heading included policies affecting college admissions, employment, government contracts, scholarships/grants, and jury selection.[25] The act's Title VII rejects the notion of preferential treatment; instead, affirmative action was supposed to create equal opportunities by eliminating barriers without granting special help to people identified as minorities. When President Lyndon Johnson signed this legislation, it was with the intention of helping protect all minorities (women included) from discrimination. However, affirmative action quickly came to be associated with a race-based preference initiative and an initiative that helped those less qualified. Soon affirmative action became associated with special treatment for Blacks. Although racial quotas were not permitted, the image of a set number of minorities receiving special privileges grew strong.[26]

As a result, many opponents of the program and conservatives have suggested that the focus of affirmative action should steer away from a race-based preference and instead should focus on structural reforms.[27] These structural reforms would focus on producing better jobs and economic opportunities for Blacks and other minorities. The expectation is that this would produce equal opportunities for all underclass groups.

One author, Joanne Barkan, refers to this structural focus as a class-based affirmative action. She notes that this proposal has a great appeal for conservatives but is problematic for several reasons, including helping too few people, not addressing class resentment, requiring radical economic reform, retaining a dependent status stigma, and giving poor Whites priority over poor Blacks numerically.[28] Explanations of these arguments follow.

A large number of the American population fall into the middle-class bracket, so many minorities who are classified as middle class would not be protected from discrimination. Income-based affirmative action would benefit poor Whites and Asians before it would help Latino and African Americans.[29] Barkan points out that resentments over class preference would still have to be addressed when, for example, middle-class students are denied college entrance in favor of a working-class student. In terms of helping underclass groups of people economically, Barkan states that the government would have to undergo massive reforms to make funds more equitable for all Americans. The likelihood of the wealthy relinquishing portions of their wealth to ameliorate economic conditions for the poor is not likely.

Advocates of affirmative action have said that the socioeconomic gap between Blacks and non-Blacks has remained too wide to abandon affirmative action. Such groups as the National Association of Minority Contractors have pointed to the need for preferences in certain career fields, stating that each time the courts eliminate another program, minority contractors go out of business.[30] In another article that debates the pros and cons of affirmative action, Cynthia Fuchs Epstein points out that affirmative action had made jobs attainable for many minorities who would have otherwise been excluded as a result of nepotism or elite buddy networks. Epstein believes that opponents of affirmative action are probably more angry about the elimination of their advantages than committed to the maintenance of a competitive market.[31]

According to Martin Kilson, another proponent of affirmative action, preferential treatment and reverse discrimination arguments do not consider a history of programs in this country that have privileged veterans, farmers, corporations, and the upper class.[32] Reparations for various groups to correct long-standing cruelties are not uncommon. In 1988, the U.S. government paid $1 billion to Japanese Americans to compensate them for their years of confinement to concentration camps and property loss during World War II. In 1971, Congress paid $1 billion and gave forty-four acres of land each to indigenous Alaskans who had been mistreated by the government. In the later part of the 1990s, Florida reportedly paid each of the nine living survivors of the 1923 Rosewood massacre, which destroyed an all-Black town, $150,000, but even now most government administrations have not supported national reparations.[33] Some have suggested that we must move from short-term compensation to long-term equality.[34]

One strong proponent of reparations, Randall Robinson, talks about "the debt" that America owes African Americans. In his book *The Debt*, Robinson discusses the setbacks African Americans have faced, such as high infant mortality rates, low income, high unemployment, below-average life span, overrepresentation in the prisons, and substandard education. He says African Americans have suffered an obstructed view of themselves due to the way they have been exploited, minimized, and manipulated throughout American history. Robinson believes America has gotten rich off of the backs of Black folks and now it's time to pay up.[35]

Although nationwide reparations to African Americans have not been seriously considered, in the late 1990s, Congress considered apologizing to African Americans for centuries of slavery. In fact, in May 1997, President Bill Clinton made a public apology, not to all Blacks, but to Black males who had been victims of the Tuskegee experiment. In the Tuskegee experiment, participating Black men were denied treatment for syphilis as part of a large government study, leaving many to die horrible and preventable deaths.[36]

In *Losing the Race*, John McWhorter writes that African Americans have to let go of the past and stop playing the victim card. He says that programs such as affirmative action only lend themselves to perpetual victimhood for Blacks. He points out that affirmative action policies in university admissions are not only obsolete but also counterproductive and disabling for young African Americans. He believes such policies do not motivate them to do their very best and compete with other top students. Although McWhorter does not say that racism is dead, he believes African Americans will be better served reinvesting in their resilience and strengths rather than their limitations.[37]

When addressing reverse discrimination, a subject some opponents of affirmative action have raised, Feagin and Feagin believe that the term *reverse discrimination* has been used to deflect attention away from large-scale problems of institutional discrimination. They point out that while anti-White discrimination was possible, it was not common on a large scale because discrimination requires both power and institutional support. Therefore, reverse discrimination would require reversing the power and resource inequalities for several hundred years. Less than forty years was not enough time to begin to make such an accusation. Only after centuries of equal hegemony could we began to classify Black privileges as reverse discrimination.[38]

In her research, Carol Swain found that Blacks and Whites are not so far apart in how they viewed affirmative action.[39] After reviewing her research, she concludes that both groups are uneasy about programs involving overt racial preferences, and both favor programs that support the disadvantaged and self-help initiatives. Although the two groups define the term *affirmative action* differently, with Whites having a more negative connotation of it, Swain notes a shift in focus by some from affirmative action to "affirmative opportunity,"[40] which might more flexibly consider both race and class factors.

Theoretical Conclusions

Sheila's clients had all experienced varying levels of discrimination. Although they felt that racism was a reality, they claimed that they did not go looking for incidents to classify as racist. The cumulative lived experiences concept is helpful in pointing out that Blacks often develop a second eye. This second eye refers to the process of looking at a potentially racist experience from a variety of different angles. The women recalled experiences in department stores in which they felt like they were being followed because they were Black. This second eye viewpoint suggests that the women would try to give merchants a benefit of the doubt, but after several experiences of being followed, they would come to the conclusion that their original inclinations were right.

The women also discussed issues of discrimination on the job. Several felt like they were treated differently by supervisors and coworkers as a result of their Blackness. While White female colleagues were perceived as being treated more delicately, these Black women felt that they were treated more like men or machines in comparison. The gendered racism concept highlights how Black women are often denied their femininity when it comes to the workplace. This treatment is due to the fact that Black women are often seen as somehow less than women in the workplace. Black women are identified as hard workers but denied any special treatments or considerations.

The women also broached the subject of surviving by overlooking certain incidents in the workplace as a means of protecting themselves and their livelihoods. And while they prided themselves in working hard to get where they were on their own merits, they still believed there was a need for such programs as affirmative action. In the next chapter, I look at how these women have remained strong in the midst of obstacles and challenges.

Notes

1. Sean Loughlin, "Race," *Gainesville Sun*, July 13, 1997, p. 7a.

2. Loughlin, "Race."

3. Jerome G. Miller, *Search and Destroy: African-American Males in the Criminal Justice System* (Cambridge, Mass.: Cambridge University Press, 1996).

4. Miller, *Search and Destroy*.

5. *San Gabriel Valley Tribune*, June 5, 2000; *Washington Spectator*, "How Bad Is It?" June 1, 1997, p. 2; Loughlin, "Race."

6. David R. Williams, "Racial Variations in Adult Health Status: Patterns, Paradoxes, and Prospects," in *America Becoming: Racial Trends and Their Consequences*, vol. 2, ed. N. Smelser, W. J. Wilson, and F. Mitchell (Washington, D.C.: National Academy Press, 2001); D. Williams, Y. Yu, J. Jackson, and N. Anderson, "Racial Differences in Physical and Mental Health: Socioeconomic Status, Stress, and Discrimination," *Journal of Health Psychology* 2, no. 3 (1997): 335–51.

7. Gloria Yamato, "Something about the Subject Makes It Hard to Name," in *Changing Our Power: An Introduction to Women's Studies*, ed. Jo Whitehouse Cochran, Donna Langston, and Carolyn Woodward (Dubuque, Iowa: Kendall Hunt, 1988), 3–6.

8. Margaret L. Andersen and Patricia Hill Collins, eds., *Race, Class, and Gender: An Anthology* (Belmont, Calif.: Wadsworth, 1995), 59–60.

9. Joe Feagin and Clairece Booher Feagin, *Racial and Ethnic Relations*, 5th ed. (Upper Saddle River, N.J.: Prentice-Hall, 1996).

10. See Daniel Patrick Moynihan, *The Negro Family* (Washington, D.C.: U.S. Department of Labor, 1965); Richard Hernstein and Charles Murray, *The Bell Curve* (New York: Free Press, 1994).

11. Joe Feagin and Heman Vera, *Living with Racism: The Black Middle Class Experience* (Boston: Beacon, 1994).

12. See Joan Morgan, *When Chickenheads Come Home to Roost: My Life as a Hip Hop Feminist* (New York: Simon & Schuster, 1999).

13. Philomena Essed, *Understanding Everyday Racism* (Claremont, Calif.: Hunter House, 1991).

14. K. Sue Jewell, *From Mammy to Miss America and Beyond: Cultural Images and the Shaping of U.S. Social Policy* (New York: Routledge, 1993), 36; see also Howard Becker, "Consciousness Industries," in *Art Worlds* (Berkeley: University of California Press, 1982).

15. Marjorie Whigham-Desire, "Fight Back," *Black Enterprise* 27 (July 1997): 62–64.

16. Feagin and Feagin, *Racial and Ethnic Relations*, 20.

17. Feagin and Feagin, *Racial and Ethnic Relations*, 20.

18. Feagin and Feagin, *Racial and Ethnic Relations*, 20.

19. Feagin and Feagin, *Racial and Ethnic Relations*, 20.

20. Philomena Essed, *Everyday Racism* (Claremont, Calif.: Hunter House, 1990), 19.

21. Essed, *Everyday Racism*, 19.

22. Howard Gardner, *Multiple Intelligences: The Theory in Practice* (New York: Basic Books, 1993); Leon Kamin, *The Science and Politics of IQ* (New York: Wiley, 1974).

23. Essed, *Understanding Everday Racism*.

24. Carol M. Swain, "Affirmative Action: Legislative History, Judicial Interpretations, Public Consensus," in *America Becoming: Racial Trends and Their Consequences*, vol. 1, ed. N. Smelser, W. J. Wilson, and F. Mitchell (Washington, D.C.: National Academy Press, 2001).

25. C. Edley Jr., *Not All Black and White: Affirmative Action and American Values* (New York: Hill & Wang, 1996), 16–17; Swain, "Affirmative Action"; Joanne Barkan, "Affirmative Action," *Dissent* 42 (1995): 461–63.

26. Virginia Held, "Affirmative Action," *Dissent* 42 (1995): 468.

27. Barkan, "Affirmative Action"; William J. Wilson, *The Truly Disadvantaged* (Chicago: University of Chicago Press, 1987).

28. Barkan, "Affirmative Action."

29. Andrew Hacker, "Affirmative Action," *Dissent* 42 (1995): 465–67.

30. Carl Hulse, "Affirmative Action Issues Not Simply Black or White," *Gainesville Sun*, July 14, 1997, pp. 1a, 4a.

31. Cynthia Fuchs Epstein, "Affirmative Action," *Dissent* 42 (1995): 464–65.

32. Martin Kilson, "Affirmative Action," *Dissent* 42 (1995): 469.

33. Marlo Roache, "Is Sorry Enough? Some Groups Push for Reparations," *Gainesville Sun*, July 15, 1997, pp. 1a, 10a.

34. Nicolaus Mills, "Affirmative Action," *Dissent* 42 (1995): 472–73.

35. Randall Robinson, *The Debt: What America Owes to Blacks* (New York: Dutton/Plume, 1999).

36. Roache, "Is Sorry Enough?"

37. John McWhorter, *Losing the Race* (New York: Perennial, 2001).

38. Feagin and Feagin, *Racial and Ethnic Relations*.

39. Swain, "Affirmative Action."

40. The term *affirmative opportunity* was coined by William J. Wilson.

CHAPTER FIVE

Standing Strong

If God is for us, who can be against us? . . . In all these things we are more than conquerors through him who loved us.

—Romans 8:31, 37, *NIV Encouragement Bible*

KIM: I remember a couple years back, I told my dad, I said—he had picked me up at the airport, right. . . . Anyway, we were driving back and I'd been thinking, and I said, "Dad, you know, I think it's just time for me to get married, you know. So-and-so likes me, so even though I don't really care about him, I can live with him [tolerate him]"—you know, that kind of thing. That's what I was saying, right.

SHEILA: Yeah.

KIM: And I was just really talking, just to see kind of what his response would be.

SHEILA: (nodding her head in agreement) Feeling him out.

KIM: Because all this stuff was going through my mind, you know—"So-and-so got married, and she got married. . . ."

SHEILA: Oh, yeah, girl, it really starts when everybody starts getting married!

KIM: It's like, maybe I have too high of expectations, so, you know, so-and-so treats me right and they got a good job or whatever, they'd be a good provider—that's good. My dad looked at me. . . . He gave me an hour sermon all the way home. "Don't you never let no pressure get to you and you just marry somebody just because they're available." . . . By the time he was finished I was wiping my eyes.

SHEILA: That's true. People will pressure you into something.

BURNADETTE: Misery loves company.

KIM: They don't tell you they gettin' slapped aside the head!

SHEILA: I get this all the time. People talking about "You're the oldest. Why aren't you married?"

KIM: Yeah, I hate that, too.

BURNADETTE: Yeah, they do that . . . but I'll tell everybody, "You better wait on God!"

In this chapter, Sheila's clients identify their support networks and ways of coping with the adversities of life. In addition, the women discuss their personal goals and dreams that they are working toward in spite of the many challenges that they face.

Family Ties

The habit of surviving concept along with the views of scholars such as Joan Morgan have dispelled the idea that Black working-class women are omnipotent superwomen. Sheila's clients confirmed this fact by stating that they saw themselves as strong but acknowledged that they drew strength from several sources to help them cope with everyday life events. A major source of empowerment for these women was their families. The women discussed the importance of maintaining close family and friend relationships to help them deal with difficult circumstances. Even though husbands and other male figures were mentioned as support resources, female familial and friendship ties were overwhelmingly mentioned as the greatest source of support. One client stated, "I have friends. I [also] have a closely knitted family, a very closely knitted family—extended family. And so I find my energy by being with my family and a few close friends." The extended family in the Black community is often called on to help nurture and raise children in both single- and two-parent homes.

Black families and communities are often the catalyst and motivation behind the successes and achievements of Black women. Black women are not just driven by career goals alone, but rather their upward mobility is often connected to lifting the image of their families and race. Many Black women are likely to feel indebted to their families and communities for their upward mobility.

A study conducted by Elizabeth Higginbotham and Lynn Weber found that Black working-class women often rely on the support of their extended families and communities, to make these advances socially and economically. In addition to family, education is seen as a vehicle to personal success. The study also found that those women who come from families that did not expect them to achieve a college education are more upwardly mobile than those who actually had college expectations.[1]

In answering the question "How do you cope with everyday stresses?" one secretary stated, "My family! If I can't talk to my family, then I'll just keep it in, or sometimes I'll start arguing or yelling when I really shouldn't. My family includes my husband, my in-laws, and then my own family." As this client noted, both the immediate family and the extended family were important to these women's support systems.

Not all of the clients had the privilege of having their extended families near them; therefore, they had to rely on other sources. One client stated, "Number one is to pray. My husband and the church are also a support. My [extended] family is such a distance from me that I don't rely on them . . . if I needed them, they would be there for me." This woman and many of the others sometimes relied on their church families and God more than on blood relatives.

Some have argued that Black extended family networks have greatly diminished, leaving a deficit of support within Black families and communities. Rose Rivers and John Scanzoni report that up until the late 1960s, Blacks were self-sufficient through the help of extended family ties.[2] Consaguineous ties supplied the individual's extrinsic needs, when he or she was not able to care for him- or herself. This interaction has been described as a type of social exchange.[3] These exchanges lend themselves to both emotional and material support. They are thought to provide a true sense of responsibility for one's fellow man within Black communities, whether related by blood or not.

It is not uncommon for these extended ties to include fictive kin, those not related by blood. A fictive relative may be a neighbor who makes sure a family has plenty to eat, a church mother who gives advice and money to the young single church members, or a good friend of the family who brings covered dishes over and frequently eats in their friends' home. Blacks who have less financially rely on this type of generalized social exchange even more, according to Rivers and Scanzoni. However, they believe that the onset of government programs such as AFDC/TANF have replaced informal sources of exchange within Black communities. The problem with this, according to Rivers and Scanzoni, is that growing numbers of Black families are becoming less and less self-sufficient and losing control of both their families and their communities. Perhaps one example of this might be a young mother on AFDC/TANF who is limited to living in unsafe neighborhoods, because she receives subsidized money to pay her rent.

In 2000, the poverty level for a family of four was just over $17,000. Although this dollar amount increased the following year, in 2001, more than thirty-two million Americans lived below the poverty level. The majority of those in poverty were Caucasian, but a large percentage of the Black population and other people of color were poor. In real numbers, in 2002, over eight million African Americans lived in poverty. This broke down to about 23 percent of the Black population living in poverty and did not include those living in near-poverty situations.[4]

Despite some of these bleak economic conditions, Dennis Hogan and his colleagues contend that Blacks are more likely to be involved in support networks than Whites, and single women more so than married women.[5] However, Sandra Hofferth believes that while Black women in particular have more interactions with their extended families, they receive minimal financial support.[6] Much of this is due to the lack of financial resources found and kept within Black families and communities. Although Blacks in the United States have a collective income of well over $300 billion annually, much of this money is going out of Black communities.[7]

With all of these points in mind, in this rapidly changing society neither single-parent families nor two-parent families can sufficiently supervise and raise their children without the influence of others. An African proverb says it best: "It takes an entire village to raise a child." African American families have followed this motto with the help of extended family, friends, and even the Black church.

K. Sue Jewell believes that Black families have been adversely affected by liberal social policies.[8] One example that Jewell cites is affirmative action. She claims that it helped some Blacks get their foot in the door but places a ceiling on their promotions. She goes on to say that such policies have raised hopes in Blacks but do not improve social or economic conditions for the majority of them.

Jewell also states that social policies that focus on extended family ties are not the answer, either, because of the lack of financial resources that inhibit their effectiveness. Black churches, according to Jewell, are the most economically independent institutions within Black communities. She estimates that even in the late 1980s, the sixty-five thousand Black churches in the United States were collectively worth over $10 billion.

In addition to the economic resources, Jewell suggests that Black churches have historically been the catalyst for prolific innovations (e.g., civil rights). Black churches have also been fruitful in providing schools, shelters, credit unions, jobs, and colleges. Jewell further notes that Black churches have encouraged cooperative sharing and mutual responsibility, the reinforcement of values and beliefs, and an avenue for cultural transmission. In the following section, I take a closer look at the role of the church and God in providing a support base for Sheila's clients.

Church and God

Asked about her support mechanisms and coping resources, Jean, who was recently married, stated, "The church is my biggest support network, besides my husband. The church is number one and then my husband, because we have no family here, so I can call [family], but sometimes you just need someone face to face. The two of them, [church and husband], are good enough for me."

Franklin Frazier states that after the emancipation of slaves, churches were called on to help freed slaves who were left without work and support.[9] He notes that Black churches are still the most important aspect of Black communities and the oldest institution in those communities. Black churches, according to Frazier, collaborate with Black families and promote responsibility and independence. It is therefore conceivable that Black churches could utilize their traditional role in communities to enhance the well-being of Black families in innovative ways.

Carla Walls notes that Black families and Black churches are interdependent and not mutually exclusive. In her study, Walls found that Black churches are often relied on by elderly Black members, whose extended family ties are not able to meet their extrinsic needs. Walls further states that Black churches have a snowball effect: they help Black elders, who in turn are able to help their children and extended families.[10]

While many clients acknowledged the role of Black churches in supporting them and acting as their pseudofamilies, a bigger emphasis seemed to be placed on the strength they gained from their belief in God. Within recent years, secular along with religious professionals in the social sciences, medical field, and the helping professions have rediscovered the importance of an individual's spirituality when looking at a person's holistic well-being. Although unaware of this trend at the time, when asked what her biggest source of support was, Sheila stated:

> My main support is "my God" that I believe in. I pray to him every day. I know I wouldn't make it through if I didn't. He keeps me grounded. Then I have my parents there. . . . Something comes up that I can't handle, I can go to them. And then I have sisters and brothers that are real close. I don't know how people make it without being close with their families. My family is my support, and like I said, there is "my God" first, and then my family.

A strong reliance on both family and God was reiterated by Sheila and several of the women. Although Sheila prided herself on being a strong, self-sufficient Black woman, she acknowledged a greater source outside herself that carried her through life's difficulties. Another woman stated:

> My biggest support, besides my family and my children, is God! Because in my relationship with him, I can move away from those stresses and get back to my seclusion with him. And having my good time with him at church, that's my greatest support . . . basically the Lord Jesus Christ, that's really my support for stressful times!

For many of these women, church and God were seen as an oasis from life's stresses as well as the pinnacle of their existence. One woman candidly stated, "I don't know how anyone else deals with it, but the only way I deal with it [life's pressures as a Black woman] is to stay in prayer, stay before the Lord, pleading and asking him to help me." As with this woman, God was often seen as a caretaker looking out for these women when no one else did.

For some of the women, prayer and faith supplemented other support mechanisms. "My support is prayer and faith," one said. "I have a few close friends that I talk to. I've been through it. I've done it all. I don't think that there is nothing that could come up that I don't feel that I can't handle. I feel that I am strong enough to go through it." Faith in God mixed with past experiences and support made some women feel like they could handle anything. After identifying herself as a Christian and a pastor's wife, Berniece stated:

> Well, mine [way of coping] will probably be different from other people's because I'm a Christian, and I know who I am. I know where I am going. And I know how I have gotten to where I am today. Nothing can take that away from me. I feel like when you're treated wrong, sometimes it's time to speak out against it, but in my case, you wait until the time is right for him [God] to speak through you. It always works out. Because sometimes we can rage, and it won't do anything, because who hears you? You have advocates for everything, but who really hears you? And so I'm strengthened, plus I have a very, very good husband. He realizes it. He's Black, too (smiling). We know the conclusion of the matter. We're Black. God made us Black, and we're going to be Black! One day it won't make no difference what color we are!

Berniece felt that God was on her side; therefore, she did not have to fight her own battles. She could wait for the right time to confront difficult situations and allow her words to be effective, rather than speaking in a rage and being ignored or locked up. She was content with her Blackness, as were most of Sheila's clients.

In addition to their families, their friends, and their faith in God, these women mentioned other ways they maintained good mental and physical health. When faced with blatant racism, one woman stated that she laughed as well as prayed to manage her anger. "I laugh! I laugh a lot. I pray and I laugh. Mostly I laugh. I laugh, and I say, 'Lord, I know you're laughing, too!' It takes laughter to deal with it, because normally you might cry." Rather than becoming outraged by social injustices, some of the women mentioned that their habit of surviving was their ability to let tension go through humor, but for others, anger seemed to work best. One client chose to scream out her problems. "To be honest, I do a little screaming," she said, laughing. "I also do a little fishing." Screaming or "talking loud," as some put it, came natural to some of these women when they were upset.

Some women chose a more direct approach to their challenges and frustrations. One client stated, "Situations that directly influence me, I have to deal with them head-on. On the general basis, I try to eat right, and I get a lot of exercise. Currently, I walk five miles a day." Assertiveness coupled with healthy habits seemed to work well for several clients.

Other clients used the support of their female friends and family. One woman stated:

> A lot of times I go back and talk to another Black female at the [police] station, and I tell her this is what happened or whatever. If I can't talk to her, I go and talk to my sister or my mom, or else I'll just say God forgive these ignorant people. You have to go through the channels before you realize, "OK, this is the one that I need to talk to."

A nurse administrator stated:

> I vent with one of my supervisors or a coworker that I have been friends with for a long time, and we kind of sneak off to the bathroom and we will vent and talk about things, and maybe we will call each other at night and have a discussion. I go on to something else [after a while] because if you dwell on things and never get past it, it will eat you up. You have to blow up, talk about it, and go on!

This client used the support of friends and colleagues to help her talk out things rather than hold things in. Getting things out in the open seemed to be helpful for many of the women and a means of survival.

A few of the women commented that they either used pressure to their advantage or did not worry at all. One client who was working on her bachelor's degree stated, "I use stress to my advantage. It makes me study more, or it makes me learn to deal with other people, including my family, who I may

not want to deal with." Another woman stated, "I really don't stress out, because stressing won't help you do anything about it. So I just pray and read
the Word [Bible]." Whether they chose to resist pressures and stress or to use
them in a constructive way, it was very obvious that these women were not
strangers to pressure and did not run from it; they knew how to both survive
it and thrive in it with the help of God and others.

Goals

In spite of some of the challenges that these women faced as African Americans, the women discussed their desires to advance in various areas of their
lives. Some expressed desires to do such things as further their educations,
own their own businesses, and help their communities. One client with older
children described her ambitions.

> I'm trying to reassess at this point. Once you get your children to a certain
> point, you say, "Well, what am I suppose to be doing now?" I have two sons that
> will be going off to college, so that brings about a change. I would like to be
> more involved in counseling, or redirect or motivate young women.

This client, as well as others with older children, was excited about the possibility of being able to pursue some of her long-desired goals. A correctional
officer stated:

> Well, right now I would like to go back to school. I only have a two-year de-
> gree. My daughter will be nineteen in April, and my biggest hope is to go back
> to school. I sometimes pray that a man will come along, sweep me off my feet,
> and send me through college, but I think I'm getting too old for that now
> (laughs). If I get it, I'm going to have to work for it, but it would be so much
> easier to go to school full-time and not have to work. That's my biggest goal,
> to go back to school.

Educating themselves and their children seemed to be a major goal for many
of Sheila's clients. In fact, some of the women took stable jobs while raising
their children, but once their duty as mothers lessened, they began to consider more risky goals. One client stated:

> My first biggest challenge, and I have accomplished this goal, was to educate my
> children. That has been a goal, and I have achieved that goal. My baby is twenty
> and she just graduated from cosmetology school. Now my next goal is to get com-
> pletely out of nursing, and I want to have a family-owned-and-operated restaurant.

When I asked this client why she wanted to leave nursing to open a
restaurant, she stated:

Well, because living in this county, there are no really good places that I have found that you can get good barbecue. There is no place that you can go and sit down and have a good soul food meal. There is no place. There are a lot of restaurants popping up, but nowhere where you can go in and eat collard greens, rice, black-eyed peas, and cornbread, and that kind of stuff. This is what I really want to do. I can cook very well.

While some goals had to do with second careers, others were more basic and related to the necessities of life. They included things that middle-class Americans often take for granted. A secretary stated:

One day eventually, I want to own my own home, because I don't own my own home right now. I want to see my children graduate from school and keep them thinking the right way. I don't have a whole lot [of goals] because I've gotten a lot of what I've wanted. I'm married. That was one of my personal goals, but I'm married and I have my own family. So now the only goal I can think of is to own my own home and be debt free. If I can get those two things, I'll be happy.

Many of the women stated that they wanted to get out of debt and be financially independent. Financial independence was particularly valued when a woman was a single parent. Sassy, who had been able to buy a home, stated:

My personal goal is to raise my daughter. I've already bought a house. When I retire, I don't want to have to worry. I want to be able to live off my savings and my retirement. If I want to go to Paris, I'll just get my ticket and go to Paris. Just be successful. When people think of me, they'll say, "Hey, she had it going on; she was smart, she was intelligent, and she got what she wanted out of life." I just don't want to have to worry when I get old, like I see a lot of old people having to worry about Social Security and having to work until they are sixty and seventy years old because there is no other way to take care of them-selves. I want to retire at the age of fifty-two!

For those women who had been successful in reaching such goals as ob-taining a higher education, buying a home, or strengthening their family re-lations, they were more than willing to share their good fortune with others in their community. An older woman stated that her goal was to help peo-ple. "My goal is not to retire. My goal is to work as long as I can, until I get my own business. When I get close to retirement, like seventy-six years of age, I want to help people in my own home—be my own boss."

When it came to goals, one grandmother was pretty content and had little to say: "That [goals], I can't talk on too much. I have grans [grandchildren], and I try to work toward their education. Right now I'm comfortable. I have everything that I want materially right now, so now I'm just trying to get closer to God. Life is too short." This client was focusing on her grandchildren's education and trying to enhance her spiritual relationship with God. Material possessions were no longer of primary interest to this client or to several others who were older and had some sense of financial security. This was also the case for another client who was not employed at the time, who stated, "My goal is to get closer to God. Material things are going to pass away!"

Several of the women placed an emphasis on long-term possessions, such as their spirits and souls, as they put it, rather than on material wealth. They believed that the things that they acquired in their lifetimes were only temporal. This belief often comforted them when they did not have all they needed monetarily.

Although they possessed a strong faith beyond the here and now, some clients wanted to do all they could *now* to help others, as noted by this client:

> My main goal in life is to do good for not only the Blacks but for the Whites and any person I come in contact with. I'm going to let people know that you and me are alive. You can be full of joy! I want people to know that in Jesus you are alive. People in the world are so burned out and pressured in everything. And [another goal is to] keep my husband happy.

Many of the women believed that when things became better for them, they needed to help someone else. Miss Mary, a retired secretary, stated that she focused on helping others rather than on receiving help.

> Right now I am retired. I'm over fifty-five, so right now I work mostly as a volunteer at the hospital, for the last six years. I don't have that much stress, because I always see someone worse than I. So my main purpose in life, now, is helping somebody else. There's a lot of things that I could have achieved in life, but now I'm comfortable. So I'm not working now; I only do volunteer work, because I'm seventy years old, so it's time for me to rest. But I tell you, I truly enjoy volunteer work.

Some of the younger women focused on goals centered around marriage and family. Priscilla, one of the clients in her twenties, stated, "I want to get married by the time I'm twenty-five and have two kids by age thirty. I also want to make between $50,000 and $70,000 a year." While to some these goals might have seemed idealistic, Priscilla was determined that she was going to meet them.

Although many of the women faced overwhelming obstacles to achieving their goals, they were determined to accomplish them and have things that would benefit them, their families, and their communities. In most cases, the goals that the women strove for, directly and indirectly, benefited others, suggesting that the women were not just interested in their own well-being but rather in the success of all those around them.

Theoretical Conclusions

The theoretical perspective that best interprets the women's coping and supportive practices in this chapter is the habit of surviving concept. The women discussed habits of surviving and maintaining a sound mind in the midst of chaos. Such habits included depending on family and friends for emotional, physical, and financial support. These women were able to find support from extended family members to help raise their children, as well as to help meet their own individual needs.

A second habit that many of these women used resourcefully was their belief in God. Their faith often resulted in regular church attendance and engaging in such acts as prayer, Bible reading, and meditation. This practice served to reduce stress levels and help the women to see the bigger picture.

Finally, the women identified humor as a way to diffuse and disarm hostile scenarios. It seemed that trivializing and ignoring comments and events helped several of the women to maintain a healthy state of mind.

Although the habit of surviving concept was useful in pointing out the survival skills of Black women, the women revealed a unique aspect of their psychological and social adjustment that was too important to ignore. This important discovery is discussed in the following section.

A Different Kind of Spirit

Throughout this book, the women share their stories, interviews, and testimonies of the hardships they have endured as working-class African American women. However, in spite of the challenges that they faced in their daily lives, the women continued to display an optimism about life and a positive outlook about who they were. Despite the detailed accounts of modern-day racism, classism, and sexism, these women possessed an outlook on life that did not lend itself to a victim mentality. Although my questions were geared toward pinpointing specific discriminations that they had experienced, these women both told me and showed me that how society defined them and how they defined themselves were two extremely different things.

After grappling with the paradox of how a person could experience racism, sexism, and classism on a daily basis yet not be defined and confined by these social stigmas throughout her day, I went back and asked the women this important follow-up question:[11] "On a scale from 0 to 100 percent, what percentage of the day do you think about racism; what percentage do you think about sexism; and what percentage do you think about classism?" I then asked them to explain why they gave those percentages (factors that contributed to those percentages and their conscious awareness of various forms of discrimination). Their overall response was quite enlightening. When it came to racism, the total average came to 27 percent. For classism, the total average was 30 percent. And, finally, for sexism, the total average was 25 percent. The critical thing that I noted when tallying their responses was that the majority of the women focused on these various forms of discrimination less than 15 percent of their day and in many cases between 0 and 10 percent of the day; however, the percentages were driven up by specific negative instances at work and in some social settings that had left a few individual response rates up at 80 and 90 percent. I found it particularly interesting that classism had the highest percentage of consideration, with sexism having the smallest consideration.

As a result of these findings and earlier observations of these women's overcoming attitudes and resilience, I needed to discover a theoretical concept that more closely described who these women were, how they saw the world, and how they saw themselves. In honor of these women and their defiant resilience, a new theoretical idea is discussed in the final chapter.

Notes

1. Elizabeth Higginbotham and Lynn Weber, "Moving Up with Kin and Community: Upward Social Mobility for Black and White Women," *Gender & Society* 6 (1992): 416–40.

2. Rose Rivers and John Scanzoni, "Social Families among African Americans: Policy Implications for Children," in *Black Children: Social, Educational & Parental Environment* (Beverly Hills, Calif.: Sage, 1995).

3. K. Sue Jewell, *Survival of the Black Family* (New York: Praeger, 1988).

4. Jesse McKinnon. *The Black Population in the United States: March 2002*, Current Population Reports, Series P20–541 (Washington, D.C.: U.S. Census Bureau, 2003).

5. Dennis Hogan, Ling-Xin Hao, and William Parish, "Race, Kin Networks, and Assistance to Mother-headed Families," *Social Forces* 68 (1990): 797–812.

6. Sandra Hofferth, "Kin Networks, Race, and Family Structure," *Journal of Marriage and the Family* 46 (1985): 791–806.

7. Valerie Lynn Gray, "Going after Our Dollar," *Black Enterprise* (July 1997): 3.

8. Jewell, *Survival of the Black Family*.

9. Franklin Frazier, *The Negro Church in America* (New York: Schocken, 1974).

10. Carla Walls, "The Role of the Church and Family Support in the Lives of Older African Americans," *Generations* 16 (1992): 33–37.

11. This follow-up question was done via telephone in early 2002. Several years had passed since the original interviews were done; therefore, not all of the women were still around/accessible for this follow-up question, but these findings represent over a third of the shop client interviewees.

CHAPTER SIX

><

Beyond Sheila's Shop:
A NEW DISCUSSION

The world is full of cactus, but we don't have to sit on it.

—Will Foley, in Paul Brownlow, *Little Bits of Wisdom*

As the women began to share their sources of strength and positive outlook on life, I became aware that these women saw themselves as more than "Black women." While it was true that they were Black and women, and that race and racial relations had a great impact on their lives, the women demonstrated that the richness of their lives transcended race, class, and gender. They chose to live their lives and enjoy their lives despite unequal and unethical social practices. They did not see themselves as constant victims of their environment or apologize for their "God-given" identities.

It therefore became apparent to me that my agenda was not necessarily their agenda. Although I wanted to confine and define their lives specifically by race, class, and gender, they expressed to me that there was more to them than these social labels, notwithstanding the fact that they were proud of who they were. Even though they had provided detailed accounts particularly of racism and sexism, they regularly commented that they did not always focus on their racial and gendered oppression, as noted in chapter 5. If they did, according to them, they would lose their minds. Instead, these women chose to focus on other more positive aspects of their lives such as their families, their goals, and their futures. Although they regularly encountered racism, classism, and sexism while living out their daily lives, *they* decided when to address these "isms" and when to let them go. This positive outlook on life is also evidenced in research that shows that African Americans have higher levels of overall mental well-being and mental health than Whites.[1]

As a result of my grappling with the fact that these women had somehow moved beyond surviving, beyond victimization, and beyond blame, I developed a theoretical concept that I felt more accurately explained their experiences and realities. This concept particularly focuses on race and gender, which were both more readily discussed by the women, identifiable from day to day, and constant unchanging factors. Although class was a real source of discrimination, like race and gender, it was the one aspect of these women's lives that could and did change, often for the better. Therefore, the concept and term that I use to explain the resilience of these women and their optimistic outlook on life is *racial and gender victorization.*

Racial and gender victorization can be defined as the ability to value one's racial and gender makeup, while not allowing social stigmas, sanctions against, or stereotypes associated with one's makeup to inhibit, diminish, or control one's self-perception, outlook, or the quality of one's everyday lived experiences. Racial and gender victorization acknowledges the fact that racial and gender inequalities vividly exist and that women of color are not always in control of external forces and outcomes of hegemonic practices. However, instead of presupposing that these women are constantly mentally and emotionally controlled internally by racist and sexist treatment, it supposes that they choose to focus on other, more positive aspects of their lives. When a perceived racist or sexist incident occurs, these women choose how they will let that experience affect them both internally and externally. To assume that these women are consumed with who is going to discriminate against them next, is to assume that they are enslaved by their racial and gender oppressors. A reactionary perspective limits the women to a mere survival existence rather than a thriving one. Instead, racial and gender victorization focuses on the empowerment of Black women. They decide what, when, and how they will let things affect them and consequently what course of action to take in response. The power is given to African American women to be racial and gender victors rather than racial and gender victims.

This paradigm change is analogous to the conceptual power of words regarding those who have survived significant atrocities such as sexual assault. A change in terms—*survivor* versus *victim*—empowers individuals to positively define and see themselves as opposed to being negatively defined by events that happened to them. Using this same example, the horrid wrongs of sexual assault are no less of an evil because the terminology has changed: different language merely separates the evil of the act from the resilience of the individual.

Negative stereotypes of African American women have been such that Black women are left with two choices: accept who society says they are, or reject this notion and live a life that is consistent with who they actually are. Jewell notes that African American women would have to reject the negative and reconstruct cultural images that positively symbolize them. In doing this, Jewell points out further, African American women would be redefining and reconstructing who they were themselves and communicating a more accurate and positive projection of themselves to the public at large using both informal and formal venues.[2] From a sociological symbolic interactionist perspective that says that who we are and how we see ourselves are shaped by our interactions and the meanings and labels we attach to them, here the women's social reconstruction of society's negative definitions of their race and gender launches them from disempowerment to empowerment. This positive reconstruction does not exonerate or call for less change from people or social institutions that have been guilty of myopic views and hegemonic practices toward working-class African American women. Rather, in addition to supporting necessary changes, it highlights the ability of these women to reinterpret themselves despite the challenges they have faced and the negative labels they have been ascribed.

Rather than rehashing what has been described by some as the pathologies, deficits, or lack within the Black community, the victorization paradigm focuses on a strengths perspective. Building from Dennis Saleebey's social work strengths perspective,[3] this theory looks at the empowerment, resilience, creativity, assets, resourcefulness, and survival skills of each of the women in this book. It provides a new lens through which we can begin to look at not only working-class African American women but also African American people in general, women of color, and people of color as a whole. And although aspects of this theoretical concept may not be applicable to men in general, the concept most definitely provides a bridge to the discourse on the strengths of African American men and men of color from a racial perspective.

Limitations of the Previous Theoretical Concepts

At the beginning of this book, I stated that the purpose of this work was to give working-class African American women a voice and a platform to describe their everyday lived experiences. Throughout each chapter, these women indeed lifted up their voices and revealed their views, highlighting these major points: their strong faith in God, a healthy dependence on familial supports, more challenges faced by race than by gender, a perception that race relations were digressing, the feeling that families as a whole were declining but that Black families and Black men needed particular support and encouragement, and despite all the odds that they faced, their capacity to thrive nevertheless.

I applied the three racial relations theoretical concepts throughout the chapters, but these concepts left room for a new theoretical concept to be developed to better explain the lived experiences of the resourceful and empowered women in Sheila's shop. Here I discuss the limitations of the three racial theories, how racial and gender victorization differs from the three racial relations concepts, and why my concept is more conducive to understanding these women and their lives.

First, the gendered racism concept focuses on the limitations of Black women's gender and race. It assumes that the status of being a Black female can result in only a constant state of oppression and subjection. Race and gender create a double burden for Black women, acting as a noose from which they could never be free. While it is true that these Black women did encounter discrimination on account of both their race and gender, this experience was not the sum total of their existence. The racial and gender victorization concept asserts that being a Black woman is not something from which one should be free but something that instead should be embraced and celebrated. And just as there are positives and negatives associated with any status, these women had experienced many more positive benefits of their racial and gender status than negative. Some of these benefits included experiencing the pride of their racial and ethnic history and traditions, finding and maintaining support within the Black sisterhood, and the widely acknowledged strength of Black matriarchal families.

The cumulative lived experiences concept focused on the responses of Blacks to an accumulation of racial discrimination over time. With it I examined how these women shared their experiences with family and friends, creating a collective memory and a collective experience of racial history. This concept proposes that repeated experiences with racism significantly affect the behavior and outlook of Black people. It rightfully suggests that it is not normally isolated events that cause Blacks to be angry toward Whites but rather a culmination of events that has left a permanent sour taste in Black peoples' mouths, causing them to explode inadvertently in seemingly the most innocuous of circumstances. While this view is largely true, and these women admitted to being keenly aware of racist incidents, they also commented on the oversensitivity of some Blacks in labeling every event or action as racist. They believed that just as years of discrimination could produce and justify negative reactions to particular experiences, years of positive experiences with Whites could produce and cultivate favorable responses.

The racial and gender victorization concept presupposes that not all racial and gender experiences are perceived as negative, and not all Whites or all males are perceived as the enemy.

The habit of surviving concept focuses on Black superwomen that live their daily lives constantly jumping over hurdles and existing in a survival mode. This view magnifies the burdens that Black women have learned to accept and cope with while trying to survive their everyday lived experiences. It proposes that Black women often learn to grin and bear their hardships like warriors, becoming apathetic about the conditions around them. The women in Sheila's shop, however, pointed out that they did not just survive but also thrived. The women admitted to difficulties and challenges, but they also identified strong support systems and goals that kept them optimistic about life and their future. They learned to depend on social networks, such as the church, their communities, families, and friends, not only to lessen their survival mode tendencies but also to allow and encourage them to be human.

As I have pointed out, the three racial relations theoretical concepts are applicable to various aspects of these women's lives; however, they do not completely capture the essence of these women's existence that could be characterized by strength, optimism, and self-determination. Resilient and resourceful, these women had tapped into a network of resources that transcended bitter experiences and made them better. They chose to be victors instead of victims. These women had experienced racial and gender victorization.

A New Point of View: Looking Ahead

So what are the implications of this study on race, class, and gender for the larger society? What can we learn from these working-class women's lives, and finally, what contribution can racial and gender victorization theory make to other studies and how we look at racial and gender issues in the broader society? To answer the first two questions, I must begin by comparing and contrasting the socioeconomic status of these working-class Black women to Black women of other classes in the broader society; then, based on race, compare them to working-class women of other races; and, finally, by gender, compare working-class Black women to their male counterparts.

When it comes to class, sociologist William J. Wilson has suggested that class is in many ways more discriminating than race.[4] David Williams and others have related this class connection to African Americans and health hazards, finding that Blacks of lower classes are more likely to be exposed at work and home to toxins, which are dumped in their neighborhoods by local government and businesses. In addition, Blacks, particularly those coming from working and lower classes, tend to lack access to preventative and curative health care, more so than Whites.[5] Class has also been linked to a host of other outcomes and effects.

Although the women did not highlight the problems associated with class in their interviews, it is clear that when they were asked which "ism" they gave the most thought to in any given day, class was it, and it definitely persisted as a powerful factor in their daily experiences and realities. Both in the media and in the literature, it is evident that many Black women who are below the poverty level are more quickly judged as unresourceful and lazy and blocked from certain opportunities and resources than even working-class Black women. Sometimes class is not accurately determinable, but a person may see a Black face that is also female and a tad unkempt, and immediately stereotypes begin to be activated and roadblocks set up. It is ironic, however, that often poor/underclass women are some of the most creative, hardworking, and resourceful people that one will ever meet. Why? Because survival is at stake—their survival as well as that of their children and families. On the one hand, they learn to enjoy the simple pleasures in life, such as relationships and life as opposed to possessions and things. Not because they don't have social and economic dreams like anyone else, but because they experience a series of ups and downs, they know that these things can go just as quickly as they come. On the other hand, these women learn to subsidize their minimum incomes with side jobs, such as braiding hair, baby-sitting, cooking, and so forth. Moreover, when the "system" fails them, they are more inclined to use nontraditional means to gain legitimate lifestyles than their working-class counterparts. Some of these means may be legal and some illegal. This is in no way meant to imply that they are less ethical than any other group, just that survival becomes the focus.

A key difference between working-class Black women and poor/underclass Black women is often based on the latter's steadily felt financial need. The working class often has more legitimate avenues to access money and livelihood than the poor/underclass, even if it's nothing more than working overtime. The desperation that the poor/underclass often experiences creates a milieu for desperate action, fulfilling the adage "Desperate people do desperate things." It is therefore imperative that we create more jobs and economic opportunities for poor/underclass people and reinstitute educational opportunities for lower classes based on low income, group underrepresentation, and first-generation college student status.

Although middle- and upper-class Black women have experienced both racism and sexism like other groups of Black women, they have been somewhat shielded from some of the challenges that come with race and gender simply because they can "afford to avoid." They certainly face racial and gender discrimination, too, but in many cases their possession and command of the all-powerful multiracial and unisex green dollar can afford them good service when a working-class or poor/underclass Black woman could not purchase this deserved fair treatment. Nevertheless, even with such buying power, education, and social connections, the idea that a middle-/upper-class Black woman can completely avoid the mistreatment associated with her race and gender is a misconception.[6] The difference, however, would be that Black women and people of color from middle/upper classes are usually more likely to confront discriminatory behavior at higher levels rather than let it go. Although working-class Black women are also bold when it comes to speaking up, sometimes economic constraints such as a potential job loss or other retaliations may inhibit this process.

In sum, Black women of all socioeconomic classes experience many of the same challenges, stereotypes, and discriminations. However, how they respond to these injustices is often indicative of their economic class. While it is evident that Black women as a whole are some of the most resourceful and resilient people that make up U.S. society, it is also evident that working-class Black women, because of their economic advantages, as compared to the poor/underclass, or their economic challenges, as compared to middle and upper classes, offer us some of the most hopeful perspectives on victorization and strength. They are not the worst off; neither have they "made it," making their midpoint perspective even more valuable.

When looking at race across the working class continuum, African American working-class women differ from working-class White women and other women of color in the following ways. First, Black women largely tend to be at the bottom of the totem pole when it comes to economic resources, at the top of the list when it comes to negative stereotypes, and lost in the median when it comes to being recognized as an empowered voice of society. Women of color as a whole, unlike most White women, tend to be in the thickets of economic displacement, especially single-parent households, and soaked in stereotypes that tend to typecast them negatively for life. However, even though other women of color experience racism and other inequities, Black women overwhelmingly tend to be identified with discrimination more than any other group.

Second, as a result of divorce, never marrying, or the high mortality rate of Black men, working-class Black women have a greater likelihood of raising a child by themselves. While these factors also affect other working-class women, statistics suggest that Black women are more likely to be affected by single-parent trends, socially, economically, and psychologically.

Third, Black women are more likely to have their femininity questioned when economic independence is sought. Black women have historically worked outside the home, from slavery to early desegregation, when it was a social norm for women to work within the home. They worked because they had to and to help their families make ends meet. As a result of their hard labor, they were often equated with men, thereby sacrificing the authenticity of their femininity when that of other women was rarely questioned. As Philomena Essed and others note, the femininity of Black women has been overlooked, exploited, or altogether denied. Black women have been idolized for their strength, loathed for their beauty, and mocked by those whose burdens they have helped carry. While it is true that a certain strength can be found among working-class women across the racial lines, working-class Black women seem to have a unique determination to thrive and not merely survive—perhaps because they have had to for centuries.

When it comes to gender, Black women hold a unique spot in society as it relates to men. Historically, they have been seen as less of a threat to the White community than Black men; however, more recently they have been perceived as not only a threat to the White community because of their double-diversity status in diversity-deprived environments, but also as a threat to their Black working-class brothers who often feel replaced by them both in the workplace and in the home. Unfortunately, Black men and Black women have been pitted against each other over the years in just about every arena, from the work world to the household, from the academic podium to the church pulpit.

Many have asked when the time will come when the antagonism between Black men and Black women is gone and neither perceives the other as a threat but rather as an ally. The women in Sheila's shop confessed that they were not archenemies with men in general, nor were they interested in competing with Black men in particular. They wanted to partner with them as a team to raise their families, strengthen their communities, and build their futures. These women were very much pro–Black men. These women showed that despite what the media depicted, Black men and women were allies and could be supportive of each other as long as they were willing to reconcile their differences.

With this being said, changes are needed to bridge gender inequalities between African American men and women. Women are still making only seventy-two cents for every dollar that a man makes. This ratio needs to be corrected not only for Black women but for women in general. Another issue is the lack of Black women in leadership roles such as clergy appointments, chief executive officers, and university presidents (or national presidents, for that matter). Still another concern is for the blaming game to stop between Black women and Black men, and for the two to begin to partner socially and economically to empower Black families, thereby improving the conditions of Black communities and society overall. As one respondent put it, "Not all men are dogs." Not all women are saints, I might add, but perhaps there is room for the two genders to work together despite past dissensions. It is only in working together that African American families, communities, and futures are collectively improved.

The final question is, Do race and gender still matter? The answer is still yes. So where does the racial and gender victorization theory take us? Hopefully it redirects our focus away from a pitiful model to powerful people. Hopefully it causes us to build on hope instead of hopelessness. One of the contributions of feminist theory is that it has sought to validate and empower the voices of the respondents that it represents, and in this venue the theoretical concept of racial and gender victorization has done just that. We must begin to see race and gender differently, no longer from the victim mentality. How do we begin to do this? We must listen, instead of assuming. We must employ the opinions of those affected by policies rather than merely implementing policies on them. We must stop blaming and begin to educate. We must stop complaining and continue to mobilize. We must take responsibility for our own lives, while seeking to improve the lives of others. We must see the can in the cannot and choose better instead of bitter. The key is aborting society's pathological model that makes everybody and everything a passive victim, and moving toward an empowerment model that actively seeks solutions for the disempowered and accountability for those with power.

If these working-class African American women have taught us anything, I hope it is the ability to see strength in the midst of stereotypes and resilience in the midst of reproach. I hope they have taught us racial and gender victorization.

Notes

1. David R. Williams, "Racial Variations in Adult Health Status: Patterns, Paradoxes, and Prospects," in *America Becoming: Racial Trends and Their Consequences*, vol. 2, ed. N. Smelser, W. J. Wilson, and F. Mitchell (Washington, D.C.: National Academy Press, 2001).

2. K. Sue Jewell, *From Mammy to Miss America and Beyond: Cultural Images and the Shaping of U.S. Social Policy* (New York: Routledge, 1993), 33.

3. Dennis Saleebey, ed., *The Strengths Perspective in Social Work Practice*, 2d ed. (White Plains, N.Y.: Longman, 1997).

4. William J. Wilson, *The Truly Disadvantaged* (Chicago: University of Chicago Press, 1987).

4. Williams, "Racial Variations," 391.

5. Joe R. Feagin and Melvin P. Sikes, *Living with Racism: The Black Middle-class Experience* (Boston: Beacon, 1994).

APPENDIX A

Interview Questions

The purpose of this study is to give working-class African American women the opportunity to describe their everyday experiences and perceptions of life in a society that constantly seeks to ascribe their existence to them. This study seeks to debunk media images and stereotypical symbols that all too often classify Black women as either welfare queens or the ambitious rivals for Black males. It attempts to allow black women to provide their own interpretations, independent of historical labels and prescribed roles.

1. What is your perception of race matters in America today?
2. What is your view of our current government?
3. How do you feel about current government policies regarding Blacks?
4. What is it like being a Black woman in America today?
5. What is your greatest struggle as a Black woman?
6. How do you cope with everyday stresses? Support networks?
7. Have you ever been discriminated against? Are you discriminated against more as a woman or as an African American?
8. Have you ever been discriminated against when it comes to housing?
9. How has racism affected you as an African American woman?
10. What barriers do you face in the job market? Employment history?
11. What is a typical day like for you?
12. Have you ever been on welfare?
13. What is your perception of women on welfare?
14. How are Black women different from White women?

15. How does the media portray Black women?
16. What are some of your personal goals?
17. How would you describe the status of Black families today?
18. What are the strengths/weaknesses in Black communities today? Biggest threat?
19. How would you describe Black women's relationship with Black men? With other Black women?
20. Who has it hardest, Black men or Black women?
21. In a word summarize the experience of African American women today.
22. Demographics:

    Age: _____
    Marital status: single, married, separated, divorced, widowed
    Number of children: _____
    Educational background: _____
    Registered voter: yes or no
    Household income: $ _____
    Religious affiliation: _____
    Housing: rent, own, other _____
    Birth origins: _____
    City of residence: _____

APPENDIX B

Demographics

Table B.1.　Age, Marital Status, Children, and Education

Interview	Age	Marital Status	Number of Children	Education
1	28	Married	1	4 years (B.A.)
2	31	Single (NM)*	0	1 year†
3	29	Divorced	1	1.5 years
4	42	Divorced	2	1 year
5	40s	Remarried‡	5	2 years
6	35	Divorced	2	4 years (B.A.)
7	43	Married	3	4 years (B.Š.)
8	36	Single (NM)	3	1 year
9	38	Divorced	0	2 years
10	33	Remarried	5	H.S.
11	46	Divorced	4	2 years (A.A.)
12	33	Divorced	1	2 years (A.A.)
13	25	Married	1	1 year
14	34	Single (NM)	0	6 years (M.A.)
15	55	Divorced	4	4 years (B.A.)
16	37	Married	3	2 years
17	52	Divorced	4	11th grade
18	70	Married	1	10th grade
19	20	Single (NM)	0	3 years
20	20	Single (NM)	0	3.5 years

* NM = never married.
† Education is represented by the number of years in college unless a high school (HS) grade level is given.
‡ Remarried status implies that the person has divorced and remarried rather than marrying again as a result of a spouse's death. Those who were listed as divorced did not indicate being remarried.

Table B.2. Voting Status, Annual Income, and Religious Affiliation

Interview	Voter	Annual Income*	Religious Affiliation
1	Yes	$45,000	Holiness†
2	Yes	$28,000	Holiness
3	Yes	$28,000	Pentecostal‡
4	Yes	$24,000	Pentecostal
5	Yes	$24,000	Holiness
6	Yes	$21,000	Pentecostal
7	Yes	$50,000	Pentecostal
8	Yes	$12,000	Holiness
9	Yes	$25,000	Baptist
10	Yes	$35,000	Pentecostal
11	Yes	$56,000	Baptist
12	Yes	$22,000	Seventh-Day Adventist
13	Yes	$20,000	Pentecostal
14	Yes	$46,000	Pentecostal
15	Yes	$23,000	Pentecostal
16	Yes	$25,000	Holiness
17	Yes	$15,000	Baptist
18	Yes	$20,000	Baptist
19	Yes	$5,000	Pentecostal
20	Yes	$0	Baptist

*Annual income is based on the total household income whether married or single. The median annual income was $23,500.
†Holiness is a sect of Pentecostalism.
‡The terms *Pentecostal* and *Holiness* are often used interchangeably in many Black Pentecostal churches.

Table B.3.   Occupations

Interview	Job/Career
1	Middle school teacher
2	Cosmetologist
3	Police officer
4	Correctional officer
5	Correctional officer
6	Middle school teacher
7	Nurse
8	Maid
9	Office clerk
10	Secretary
11	Nurse administrator
12	Correctional officer
13	Not recorded
14	Elementary school teacher
15	Social worker
16	Not employed
17	Packaging worker
18	Retired secretary
19	Full-time student
20	Full-time student

Table B.4.   Percentage of Time Consumed with Racism, Classism, and Gender

	Race	Class	Gender
	35	45	20
	10	0	0
	15	20	7
	80	7	90
	30	80	50
	15	60	5
	5	0	0
Average:	27	30	25

Note: A telephone follow-up question was conducted January 24 through February 6, 2002; responses here are based on daily perception. A third of the constituents answered this question; due to the time lapse of several years, not all interviewees could be located to answer this question.

APPENDIX C

Methods

The data were transcribed and separated by categories corresponding to an interview question:

- Race matters
- Views of current government
- Government policies regarding Blacks
- The experience of being a Black woman
- Greatest struggle
- Coping with stress/support networks
- Cases of discrimination
- Effects of racism
- Barriers on the job
- Typical day
- Ever on welfare
- Difference between Black and White women
- Media and Black women
- Goals
- Views of Black families
- Strengths and weaknesses and threats in Black communities
- Who has it hardest
- One word

After the data were separated by categories, quotes from the women were organized according to interviewee. Variations of responses were noted for each woman. Similarities and differences were also noted, and representative responses were cited in the text.

The Extended Case Method

In reviewing the content of my interviews and observations, I used the extended case method to examine the application of three racial relations concepts. The extended case method, according to Michael Burawoy, "seeks generalization through reconstructing existing generalizations, that is, the reconstruction of existing theory."[1] Simply stated, this method constructs new theory from existing theory. Unlike grounded theory,[2] which seeks to discover new theory by abstracting phenomenon from time and place (it builds theory from the ground up), the extended case method focuses on revising applicable existing theory (it applies and refines existing theory to better fit the current phenomenon). Instead of trying to explain a phenomenon with existing theory, the extended case method allows the phenomenon to help create new theory.

In this study, the emphasis of the extended case method was not on numerical statistical significance, such as large random sample sizes, but on societal significance. The extended case method was used to focus on the significance that could be found in what these twenty interviews (micro) told me about the larger social environment (macro) in which these women lived.

I applied the extended case method by first examining the three previously mentioned racial relations theoretical concepts and considering their usefulness in addressing my research questions. In the final chapter, however, I applied a new theory based on data that I gathered from the respondents, after reviewing the limitations of the existing theories.

Notes

1. Michael Burawoy, *Ethnography Unbound* (Berkeley: University of California Press, 1991), 279.

2. Barney G. Glaser and Anselm L. Strauss, *The Discovery of Grounded Theory* (New York: Aldine de Gruyter, 1967).

Bibliography

Allison, Paul, and Frank Furstenberg. "How Marital Dissolution Affects Children: Variations by Age and Sex." *Developmental Psychology* 25 (1989): 540–49.

Andersen, Margaret L., and Patricia Hill Collins, eds. *Race, Class, and Gender: An Anthology*. Belmont, Calif.: Wadsworth, 1995.

Bailey, Kenneth D. *Methods of Social Research*. 4th ed. New York: Free Press, 1994.

Banks, Ingrid. *Hair Matters: Beauty, Power, and Black Women's Consciousness*. New York: New York University Press, 2000.

Barkan, Joanne. "Affirmative action." *Dissent* 42 (1995): 461–63.

Bartky, Sandra. *Femininity and Domination: Studies in the Phenomenology of Oppression*. New York: Routledge, 1990.

Becker, Howard. *Art Worlds*. Berkeley: University of California Press, 1982.

Bell, Derrick. *Faces at the Bottom of the Well*. New York: Basic Books, 1992.

Benjamin, Lois. *The Black Elite: Facing the Color Line in the Twilight of the Twentieth Century*. Chicago: Nelson-Hall, 1991.

Berardo, Felix. Family Research in the 1980s: Recent Trends and Future Directions." In *Contemporary families*, ed. Alan Booth. Minneapolis: National Council on Family Relations, 1990.

Bernstein, Jared. "Rethinking Welfare Reform." *Dissent* 40 (Summer 1993): 277–79.

Blum, Linda M., and Theresa Deussen. Negotiating Independent Motherhood: Working-class African American Women Talk about Marriage and Motherhood." *Gender & Society* 10 (1996): 199–211.

Bray, Rosemary. "Taking Sides against Ourselves." *New York Times Magazine* 141 (November 17, 1991): 56ff.

Brownlow, Paul C., ed. "Will Foley #95." In *Little Bits of Wisdom*. Fort Worth, Tex.: Brownlow, 1993.

Burawoy, Michael. *Ethnography Unbound*. Berkeley: University of California Press, 1991.

Byrd, Ayana, and Lori Tharps. *Hair Story: Untangling the Roots of Black Hair in America*. New York: St. Martin's, 2001.

Caputo, Richard. "Family Poverty, Unemployment Rates, and AFDC Payments: Trends among Blacks and Whites." *Families in Society: The Journal of Contemporary Human Services* 74 (1993): 515–25.

Carmichael, Stockley, and Charles Hamilton. *Black Power*. New York: Vintage, 1967.

Coontz, Stephanie. *The Way We Never Were*. New York: Basic Books, 1992.

Cose, Ellis. *The Rage of a Privileged Class*. New York: HarperCollins, 1993.

Cowan, Philip. "The Sky is Falling, but Popenoe's Analysis Won't Help Us Do Anything about It." *Journal of Marriage and the Family* 55 (1993): 548–52.

Cowan, Philip, and Carolyn Cowan. *When Partners become Parents*. New York: Basic Books, 1992.

Cowen, Emory L., Ellis L. Gesten, Mary Boike, Pennie Norton, Alice B. Wilson, and Michael A. DeStefano. "Hairdressers as Caregivers: A Descriptive Profile of Interpersonal Help-giving Involvements." *American Journal of Community Psychology* 7 (1979): 633–48.

Cox, Frank. *Human Intimacy*. 7th ed. St. Paul, Minn.: West, 1996.

Cox, Oliver. *Caste, Class, and Race*. Garden City, N.Y.: Doubleday, 1948.

Crittendon, Denise. "Who's Minding the Store—Asians or African-Americans? *The Crisis* 101 (1994): 26–29.

Davis, Liane, and Jan Hagen. "Stereotypes and Stigma: What's Changed for Welfare Mothers." *Affilia* 11 (1996): 319–37.

Davis, Richard. *The Black Family in a Changing Black Community*. New York: Garland, 1993.

DuBois, W. E. B. *The Souls of Black Folk*. New York: Fawcett, 1961.

Duneier, Mitchell. *Slim's table*. Chicago: University of Chicago Press, 1992.

Eayrs, Michelle A. "Time, Trust and Hazard: Hairdressers' Symbolic Roles." *Symbolic Interaction* 16 (1993): 19–37.

Edley, C., Jr. *Not All Black and White: Affirmative Action and American Values*. New York: Hill & Wang, 1996.

Edwards, Audrey. "Programs that Work: Looking Good . . . Inside and Out." *Essence* 27 (April 1997): 50.

Empey, La Mar, and Mark Stafford. *American Delinquency*. Belmont, Calif.: Wadsworth, 1982.

Epstein, Cynthia Fuchs. "Affirmative Action." *Dissent* 42 (1995): 464–65.

Essed, Philomena. *Everyday Racism*. Claremont, Calif.: Hunter House, 1990.

———. *Understanding Everyday Racism*. Newbury Park, Calif.: Sage, 1991.

Feagin, Joe R. "America's Welfare Stereotypes." *Social Science Quarterly* 52 (1972): 921–33.

Feagin, Joe R., and Clairece Booher Feagin. *Racial and Ethnic Relations*. 5th ed. Upper Saddle River, N.J.: Prentice Hall, 1996.

Feagin, Joe R., and Melvin P. Sikes. *Living with Racism: The Black Middle-class Experience.* Boston: Beacon, 1994.

Feagin, Joe R., and Hernan Vera. *White Racism: The Basics.* New York: Routledge, 1995.

Frazier, Franklin. *The Negro Church in America.* New York: Schocken 1974.

Freedman, Rita. *Beauty Bound.* Lexington, Mass.: Lexington, 1986.

Friedan, Betty. *The Feminine Mystique.* New York: Norton, 1963.

Frye, Marilyn. *The Politics of Reality.* Trumansburg, N.Y.: Crossing, 1983.

Gardner, Howard. *Multiple Intelligences: The Theory in Practice.* New York: Basic Books, 1993.

Gimlin, Debra. "Pamela's Place: Power and Negotiation in the Hair Salon." *Gender & Society* 10 (1996): 505–26.

Glaser, Barney G., and Strauss, Anselm L. *The Discovery of Grounded Theory.* New York: Aldine de Gruyter, 1967.

Glasgow, Douglas G. *The Black Underclass: Poverty, Unemployment and Entrapment of Ghetto Youth.* San Francisco: Jossey-Bass, 1980.

Glazer, Nathan. *Affirmative Discrimination.* New York: Basic Books, 1975.

Goodban, Nancy. "The Psychological Impact of Being on Welfare. *Social Service Review* 59 (1985): 403–22.

Gray, Valerie Lynn. "Going after Our Dollar." *Black Enterprise* (July 1997): 3.

Greene, Beverly. African American Families: A Legacy of Vulnerability and Resilience." In *Annual Editions Marriage and Family 1999/2000.* Guilford, Conn.: Dushkin/McGraw-Hill, 1999.

Hacker, Andrew. "Affirmative Action." *Dissent* 42 (1995): 465–67.

Halbwachs, Maurice. *The Collective Memory.* New York: Harper & Row, 1980.

Hallpike, C. R. "Social Hair." In *Comparative Religion: An Anthropological Approach,* ed. William Lessa and Evon Z. Vogt (pp. 99–104). New York: Harper & Row, 1972.

Held, Virginia. "Affirmative Action." *Dissent* 42 (1995): 468.

Helmbold, Lois Rita. "Writing the History of Black and White Working Class Women." *Women's Studies* 17 (1989): 37–48.

Herbert, Bob. "The Real Welfare Cheats." *New York Times,* April 26, 1996.

Hernstein, Richard, and Charles Murray. *The Bell Curve.* New York: Free Press, 1994.

Higginbotham, Elizabeth, and Lynn Weber. "Moving Up with Kin and Community: Upward Social Mobility for Black and White Women. *Gender & Society* 6 (1992): 416–40.

Hofferth, Sandra. "Kin Networks, Race, and Family Structure." *Journal of Marriage and the Family* 46 (1985): 791–806.

Hogan, Dennis, Ling-Xin Hao, and William Parish. "Race, Kin Networks, and Assistance to Mother-headed Families." *Social Forces* 68 (1990): 797–812.

hooks, bell. *Yearning: Race, Gender, and Cultural Politics.* Boston: South End, 1990.

Hulse, Carl. "Affirmative Action Issues Not Simply Black or White." *Gainesville Sun,* July 14, 1a, 4a.

Jackman, Mary. *The Velvet Glove.* Berkeley: University of California Press, 1994.

Jarrett, Robin L. "Living Poor: Family Life among Single Parent, African American Women. *Social Problems* 41 (1994): 30–49.

———. "Welfare Stigma among Low-income African American Single Mothers." *Family Relations* 45 (1996): 368–74.

Jewell, K. Sue. *Survival of the Black Family*. New York: Praeger, 1988.

———. *From Mammy to Miss America and Beyond: Cultural Images and the shaping of U.S. Social Policy*. New York: Routledge, 1993.

Jones, Lisa. *Bulletproof Diva: Tales of Race, Sex, and Hair*. New York: Doubleday, 1994.

Kamin, Leon. *The Science and Politics of IQ*. New York: Wiley 1974.

Karger, Howard J., and David Stoesz. *American Social Welfare Policy: A Pluralist Approach*. 3d ed. New York: Longman, 1998.

Kilson, Martin. "Affirmative Action." *Dissent* 42 (1995): 469.

Krikorian, Michael. "Central Los Angeles: Along with Mousse, Salon Offers AIDS and Cancer Advice." *Los Angeles Times*, May 16, 1997, 5.

Ladner, Joyce A. *Tomorrow's Tomorrow: The Black Woman*. Garden City, N.Y.: Doubleday, 1971.

Loughlin, Sean. "Race." *Gainesville Sun*, July 13, 1997, 7a.

Macionis, John J. *Sociology*. 6th ed. Upper Saddle River, N.J.: Prentice Hall, 1997.

Marx, Karl, and Friedrich Engels. *The Communist Manifesto*. Oxford: University Press, 1848.

———. *The German Ideology*. New York: Lawrence & Wishart, 1970.

McBride, Angela, and William McBride. "Theoretical Underpinnings for Women's Health. *Women and Health* 6 (1981): 37–55.

McKinnon, Jesse. *The Black Population in the United States: March 2002*. Current Population Reports, Series P20–541. Washington, D.C.: U.S. Census Bureau, 2003.

McWhorter, John. *Losing the Race: Self-sabotage in Black America*. New York: Perennial, 2001.

Miller, Jerome G. *Search and Destroy: African-American Males in the Criminal Justice System*. Cambridge, Mass.: Cambridge University Press, 1996.

Mills, Nicolaus. "Affirmative Action." *Dissent* 42 (1995): 472–73.

Morgan, Joan. *When Chickenheads Come Home to Roost: My Life as a Hip Hop Feminist*. New York: Simon & Schuster, 1999.

Mori, Aisha. "Letting Their Hair Down." *San Gabriel Valley Weekly*, June 8, 2001, 8.

Morrow, Willie L. *400 Years without a Comb*. San Diego, Calif.: Morrow, 1973.

Moynihan, Daniel Patrick. *The Negro Family*. Washington, D.C.: U.S. Department of Labor, 1965.

Murray, Charles. *Losing Ground: American Social Policy, 1950–1980*. New York: West, 1984.

Newman, David. *Sociology of Families*. Thousand Oaks, Calif.: Pine Forge, 1999.

NIV Encouragement Bible: New International Version. 2001. Joni Eareckson Tada and Dave and Jan Dravecky (general editors). Grand Rapids, Mich.: Zondervan, 2001.

Oldenburg, Ray. *The Great Good Place: Cafes, Coffee Shops, Community Centers, Beauty Parlors, General Stores, Bars, Hangouts and How They Get You Through the Day*. New York: Paragon House, 1989.

Orlean, Susan. "Short Cuts." New Yorker 71 (May 1, 1995): 42–47.

Owens, Darryl E. "Hair care comes with prayers." Orlando Sentinel, April 22, 2000, D1, D8.

Perkins, John. A Call to Holistic Ministry. Arlington, Va.: Open Door, 1981.

Popenoe, David. "American Family Decline, 1960–1990: A Review and Appraisal." Journal of Marriage and the Family 55 (1993): 527–41.

Poppendieck, Janet. Sweet charity. New York: Viking,1998.

Quadagno, Jill. The Color of Welfare: How Racism Undermines the War on Poverty. New York: Oxford University Press, 1994.

Rank, Mark. Living on the edge: The Realities of Welfare in America. New York: Columbia University Press, 1994.

Raschke, Helen. "Divorce." In Handbook of Marriage and the Family, ed. Marvin Sussman and Suzanne Steinmetz. New York: Plenum, 1987.

Rivers, Rose, and John Scanzoni. "Social Families among African-Americans: Policy Implications for Children." In Black Children: Social, Educational & Parental Environments. Beverly Hills, Calif.: Sage, 1995.

Roache, Marlo. "Is Sorry Enough? Some Groups Push for Reparations." Gainesville Sun, July 15, 1997, 1a, 10a.

Robinson, Randall. The debt: What America owes to blacks. New York: Dutton/Plume, 1999.

Rooks, Noliwe M. Hair Raising: Beauty, Culture, and African American Women. New Brunswick, N.J.: Rutgers University Press, 1996.

Rubin, Lillian. Families on the Fault Line: America's Working Class Speaks about the Family, the Economy, Race, and Ethnicity. New York: HarperCollins, 1994.

Saleebey, Dennis, ed. The Strengths Perspective in Social Work Practice. 2d ed. White Plains, N.Y.: Longman, 1997.

Saluter, Arlene. "Marital Status and Living Arrangements: March, 1993." In Bureau of the Census Current Population Reports (p. 20). Washington, D.C.: U.S. Government Printing Office, 1994.

San Gabriel Valley Tribune. June 5, 2000.

Schaefer, Richard. Racial and Ethnic Groups. 3d ed. Glenview, Ill.: Scott, Foresman, 1988.

Scott, Kesho Yvonne. The Habit of Surviving: Black Women's Strategies for Life. New Brunswick, N.J.: Rutgers University Press, 1991.

Seccombe, Karen, Delores James, and Kimberly Battle-Walters. "They Think You Ain't Much of Nothing: The Social Construction of the Welfare Mother." Journal of Marriage and the Family 60 (1998): 849–65.

Shakespeare, Tonia L. "Hairy Situation, Profitable Business: Black-owned Salons Are Gaining Financial Clout in the Ethnic Consumer Market." Black Enterprise 25 (1995): 31–32.

Simon, Diane. Hair Public, Political, Extremely Personal. New York: St. Martin's, 2000.

Sloane, Leonard. "Black Women's Hair Care: Market's There, and Now So Are the Appliances." New York Times, August 15, 1992, 16, 46.

St. Jean, Yanick, and Joe R. Feagin. Double Burden: Black Women and Everyday Racism. Armonk, N.Y.: Sharpe, 1997.

Stacey, Judith. "Good Riddance to the Family: A Response to Popenoe." *Journal of Marriage and the Family* 55 (1993): 545–47.

Staples, Robert, ed. *The Black Family: Essays and Studies.* 3d ed. Belmont, Calif.: Wadsworth, 1988.

Strong, Bryan, and Christine DeVault. *The Marriage and Family Experience.* 6th ed. St. Paul, Minn.: West, 1995.

Sullivan, Thomas, and Kenrick Thompson. 1994. *Introduction to Social Problems.* 3d ed. New York: Macmillan, 1994.

Swain, Carol M. "Affirmative Action: Legislative History, Judicial Interpretations, Public Consensus." In *America Becoming: Racial Trends and Their Consequences,* vol. 1, ed. N. Smelser, W. J. Wilson, and F. Mitchell. Washington, D.C.: National Academy Press, 2001.

Tannen, Mary. "The Village Barber." *New York Times Magazine* (November 20, 1994): 101–2.

Tucker, M. B., and R. J. Taylor. "Demographic Correlates of Relationship Status among Black Americans." *Journal of Marriage and the Family* 51 (1989): 655–65.

U.S. Census Bureau. *Census 2000 Summary File 4 (SF4) Sample Data.* Washington, D.C.: U.S. Government Printing Office, 2000.

———. *Current Population Reports: Money Income in the United States: 1999.* Washington, D.C.: U.S. Government Printing Office, 2000.

U.S. Census of Population and Housing for Florida. Washington, D.C.: U.S. Department of Commerce, Economics and Statistics Administration, Bureau of Census, 1990.

Walls, Carla. "The Role of the Church and Family Support in the Lives of Older African-Americans. *Generations* 16 (1992): 33–37.

Washington Spectator. "How Bad Is It?" June 1, 1997, 2.

Wattenberg, Ben, and Richard Scammon. "Black Progress and Liberal Rhetoric." *Commentary* (April 1973): 35.

Whigham-Desire, Majorie. "Fight back. *Black Enterprise* 27 (July 1997): 62–64.

Wiesenfeld, Alan R., and Herbert M. Weis. "Hairdressers and Helping: Influencing the Behavior of Informal Caregivers." *Professional Psychology* 10 (1979): 786–92.

Williams, D., Y. Yu, J. Jackson, and N. Anderson. "Racial Differences in Physical and Mental Health: Socioeconomic Status, Stress, and Discrimination. *Journal of Health Psychology* 2, no. 3 (1997): 335–51.

Williams, David R. "Racial variations in Adult Health Status: Patterns, Paradoxes, and Prospects." In *America Becoming: Racial Trends and Their Consequences,* vol. 2, ed. N. Smelser, W. J. Wilson, and F. Mitchell. Washington, D.C.: National Academy Press, 2001.

Williams, Louis. "Dennis': The Relationship between a Black Barbershop and the Community That Supports It." *Human Mosaic* 27 (1993): 29–33.

Wilson, Midge, and Kathy Russell. *Divided Sisters: Bridging the Gap between Black Women and White Women.* New York: Doubleday, 1996.

Wilson, Patricia, and Ray Pahl. "The Changing Sociological Construct of the Family." *Sociological Review* 36 (1988): 233–72.

Wilson, William J. *The Truly Disadvantaged*. Chicago: University of Chicago Press, 1987.

———. *When Work Disappears: The World of the New Urban Poor*. New York: Knopf, 1996.

———. *The Bridge over the Racial Divide: Rising Inequality and Coalition Politics*. Berkeley: University of California Press, 1999.

Wright, Earl. "More than Just a Haircut: An Ethnographic Study of an Urban African American Barbershop. Master's thesis, University of Memphis, 1997.

Yamato, Gloria. "Something about the Subject Makes It Hard to Name. In *Changing Our Power: An Introduction to Women's Studies*, ed. Jo Whitehorse Cochran, Donna Langston, and Carolyn Woodward (3–6). Dubuque, Iowa: Kendall-Hunt, 1988.

Index

weave. *See* hair styles
welfare: Aid to Families with
    Dependent Children (AFDC),
    41, 44–45, 95; and the media,
    80; Temporary Assistance to

Needy Families (TANF),
41–43
working class: African American
    families, 64; Black women, 109–11;
    description, 5

About the Author

Kimberly Battle-Walters, Ph.D., is an associate professor in social work at Azusa Pacific University in Azusa, California. She received her master's degree in social work from Temple University and a Ph.D. in sociology from the University of Florida with an emphasis in race and family. Dr. Battle-Walters has provided service in six of the seven continents of the world and is a Fulbright alum to South Africa. She has published several works on African American matters, welfare reform, women's concerns, and international issues.